Key Stage 3

Religious Education Directory

Source *to* Summit

Year 7

T0347352

SERIES EDITOR
Andy Lewis

Rebecca Jinks
Laura Skinner-Howe
Mateusz Boniecki
Ann-Marie Bridle

OXFORD
UNIVERSITY PRESS

OXFORD
UNIVERSITY PRESS

Great Clarendon Street, Oxford, OX2 6DP, United Kingdom

Oxford University Press is a department of the University of Oxford. It furthers the University's objective of excellence in research, scholarship, and education by publishing worldwide. Oxford is a registered trade mark of Oxford University Press in the UK and in certain other countries.

British Library Cataloguing in Publication Data
Data available

978-1-38-203632-0

978-1-38-203630-6 (ebook)

10 9 8 7 6 5 4 3 2

The manufacturing process conforms to the environmental regulations of the country of origin.

Printed in the United Kingdom by Bell & Bain Ltd, Glasgow

Nihil obstat: Philip Robinson, Censor Deputatus

Imprimatur + Bernard Longley, Archbishop of Birmingham

17th May 2023

The Nihil obstat and Imprimatur are a declaration from the Catholic Church that the parts of this publication concerned with doctrine and morals are free from error. It is not implied that those who have granted the Nihil obstat and Imprimatur agree with the contents, opinions or statements expressed.

FSC
www.fsc.org

MIX
Paper | Supporting
responsible forestry
FSC® C007785

This resource is officially endorsed and meets the requirements of the *Religious Education Directory: To Know you More Clearly*. The Catholic Education Service has reviewed this resource and confirms that: it meets the expected outcomes for the relevant age-phase covered by this resource; it provides an age-related sequence of learning that enables all pupils to make progress in religious education; it ensures pupils are developing each of the three ways of knowing (understand, discern, respond) at all points in their learning; it gives appropriate weight to each of the knowledge lenses, allowing pupils to make meaningful connections between scriptural texts (hear), Catholic beliefs (believe), prayer and liturgy (celebrate) and the relationship of faith to life (live); as part of the live lens it provides students with the study of a rich mix of philosophical and ethical issues, artistic expression, and lived religion elements in each year of their study; it is reflective of the global nature of Catholicism and is inclusive of the diverse cultural expressions of Catholic faith and life; it presents learning in an age-appropriate sequential way designed to maximise progress.

This endorsement comes as part of a process approved by the Department of Catholic Education and Formation of the Catholic Bishops Conference of England and Wales.

CONTENTS

In Chapters 1 to 5, students can choose to study **any two** of the Ethical, Lived Religion and Artistic Expression Options.

INTRODUCTION

Welcome to the first book in the *Source to Summit* series. The team who have worked on this book are excited to begin a three-year, three-book journey with you as you learn all about the story of the Bible, the story of Christianity and the story of the Church today. This book has been written to make every student feel comfortable and welcomed into this story – whether you are Catholic yourself, or studying this story as a member of a Catholic school.

Source to Summit

We have used a play on words for our title. It is based on a quote from the Catechism of the Catholic Church which describes the Eucharist as 'the source and summit of the Christian life' (CCC 1324). We wanted to highlight the journey that is at the heart of this book, which is the story of the Church from the source – the very moment of creation – to the complete and full revelation found in Jesus Christ, and then on to how the early Church was established, eventually becoming the vibrant faith that is practised today by around 1.3 billion Catholics all over the world.

We will look at how the ancient stories told in the Bible continue to influence how modern Catholics live their lives today, guiding how they choose to live and interact with the world and with others. We will look at how they have inspired artists to try to express and communicate their feelings about God to others. As well as learning about these stories you will be encouraged to reflect on their meaning and how they might fit with your own beliefs and values.

The Bible and other key books

You will learn more about the Bible, the key text of the Christian faith – how it was written, and how it has been translated and interpreted. In this book we have used a translation called the English Standard Version – Catholic Edition. It is this translation of the Bible that will be used in the new Lectionary, a Catholic book containing portions of the Bible to be read on particular days of the year. It will therefore be the version used for the readings in Mass.

We have included quotes from the Bible, with their references. For a fuller understanding, we would encourage you to look up the reference in your class Bible, and to read around the quotes to understand them in context.

We also quote and refer to:

CCC – the *Catechism of the Catholic Church*, a book that summarises the beliefs of the Church.

YC – the *Youth Catechism of the Catholic Church* or *YOUCAT,* a version of the Catechism written to help young people better understand the beliefs of the Church.

Dialogue and Encounter

Chapter 6 will look at how the Catholic Church enters into dialogue (discussion and debate) with other Christian denominations. In the school year, there will be time for you to study other major religions and worldviews. Your teacher should be able to find resources that cover those religions outside of this book.

How to use this book

We have tried to make the books in this series as easy to use as possible.

Each chapter is introduced with an **overview** of the big ideas and questions that you will cover in your lessons for that half-term.

We have written each **title** as a question to help you work out the main enquiry or focus for the lesson.

Each double-page lesson has a clear **objective** so you can know exactly what you are trying to achieve.

We will often quote from the Bible or Catechism. Sometimes we will use callout boxes to help you understand the **quotations**.

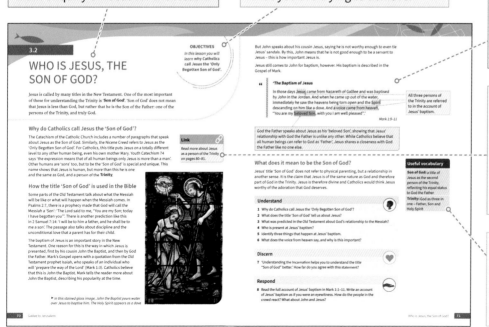

Throughout the book, and during Key Stage 3, you will return to ideas and topics again and again. These **links** will help you to make connections so you can build on what you have learned.

We have given definitions for **useful vocabulary** to help you understand the text. Test yourself on these key words to make sure you know what they mean.

There are three types of activity in each lesson.

Understand

These questions check that you have understood what you have learned.

Discern

These questions encourage you to judge wisely. For example, they might ask to you look at different points of view, decide which you agree with more, and explain your reasons for making that judgment.

Respond

These questions allow you to reflect on what you have learned and to consider how this learning fits with your own personal viewpoint. You might consider whether what you have learned will have an impact on how you live and act.

At the end of each chapter you can use these **Assessment** pages to test yourself on what you have learned.

This simple **Key vocabulary** quiz will check that you have understood and remembered the key terms from this chapter.

The questions in this **Knowledge check** quiz get progressively more difficult as you work through them.

This **Extended writing activity** sets a big question for you to practise your writing skills. We have included some advice to help you structure and complete your answer.

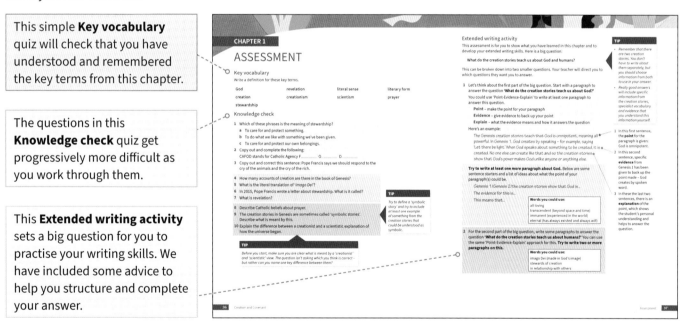

The activities and Assessment pages in the book will help you to check that you are learning, understanding and remembering the story from *Source to Summit*, which is the central story of the Catholic Church. We hope you enjoy using this book in your RE lessons this year.

Andy Lewis
RE Teacher and Series Editor

CREATION AND COVENANT

Introduction

Have you ever asked yourself what caused the universe, or why we are on this earth?

Questions about where the universe came from and the meaning of life have fascinated people for as long as humans have lived. Catholics, like many religious people, believe that God can help us to understand these questions because they believe that **God made the universe and everything in it**. Scientists believe that the Big Bang theory and the theory of evolution give evidence that can help to answer these questions. Sometimes people think that science and religion disagree but this isn't necessarily the case. **The Catholic Church believes that science and religion can help to give the fullest and best answer to these big questions by working together** – many scientists who have a religious faith believe the same.

In this chapter we are going to consider how creation is at the heart of God's relationship with humans. Catholics believe that God chose to create because God is loving, and that God created only goodness because God is all loving. **Catholics believe that God created humans to have a relationship with them**. **This story of God loving, creating and sustaining the world is vital to Catholics.** It is awe inspiring, leading Catholics to worship God and create beautiful poetry, literature and art to express this incredible work of God.

The creation stories in the Bible give important teachings to Catholics about the value of human life and caring for the world. Who would imagine that stories that are thousands of years old can give us teachings that can guide us in the twenty-first century? The world is facing an environmental crisis. **In the creation stories, Catholics are told to care for the earth as stewards.** We can see injustice and inequality in the world. **In the creation stories, Catholics are told that humans are created in God's image and that human life is precious and to be cared for.** These important messages motivate and inspire Catholics to try to improve the world, so that the world we live in, and all the people in it, can be cared for in the way that God intended.

HOW DO WE KNOW ABOUT GOD?

OBJECTIVE

*In this lesson you will learn about **how God is revealed to humans.***

Catholics believe in **God**, who is the **Trinity**: the Father, the Son and the Holy Spirit. Their faith in God shapes their lives and so Catholics believe that it is important to listen to the different ways in which God speaks to them so that they can become closer to God, and live in the way that God calls them to live.

What do Catholics mean by the word 'revelation'?

Revelation is when we come to know something or someone we did not know before. For Catholics, revelation means the ways in which God is made known to people, such as through showing God's qualities. This is most perfectly done through Jesus, who Catholics believe was God in human form.

Catholics believe that humans can come to know God in different ways.

- One way is by using reason (our ability to think) to find God in the world around us, or by thinking about what it means to be human. For example, seeing how well-designed and beautiful the world seems to be might lead someone to believe in a God who has designed it. Or you might believe God is made known to people when they are guided to do good deeds by God.
- There are some things that humans could never come to know without God's help. This is why the second kind of revelation is called divine revelation. This might happen through reading the word of God in the Bible or through the teaching of the Church (known as tradition).

▼ *For some people, looking at the astonishing beauty of the world is one way that God can be made known to humans*

The Bible as a form of revelation

The holy book for Catholics and all Christians is the Bible. Christians believe that the Bible is the word of God, meaning that it is how God speaks to them. This means that the people who wrote down God's word in the Bible were guided by the Holy Spirit to do this so that the Bible could be trusted.

Christians believe that they can grow closer to God through reading the Bible – the words of the Bible can help them to become the person that God has made them to be. Therefore, the Bible can help someone to have a better relationship with God.

Useful vocabulary

God: the one supreme being, who creates and sustains everything

Trinity: God as three in one – Father, Son and Holy Spirit

What is in the Bible?

The Bible is divided into two main parts: the Old Testament and the New Testament.

Old Testament

- This part of the Bible was written before Jesus' life.
- It contains the history and faith of the Jewish people. Christianity grew out of Judaism. The first followers of Jesus were all Jews who would have known what we now call the Old Testament as their scriptures.

New Testament

- This part of the Bible was written after Jesus' life.
- It contains accounts of the life, ministry, death and resurrection of Jesus and the early history and faith of those who followed Jesus, who we call Christians.

The meaning of the word 'testament' is **covenant**, which is an agreement or promise. The whole of the Bible is related to the covenants made between God and humans. The covenants reveal that God wants to enter into a relationship with humans, to guide and help them, showing that God is good and faithful.

In the Old Testament, Catholics read about how God made covenants with people who placed their faith in God, such as Abraham and Moses. Later in the Old Testament, they read about how kings such as Solomon and prophets such as Deborah listened carefully to God and how they were guided by God.

The central figure in the New Testament is Jesus, the Son of God. The covenant in the New Testament builds on the Old Testament. In the New Testament, God is revealed fully in Jesus, meaning that the people who met Jesus, met God, helping people to know God's revelation better.

How do Catholics hear God's voice in the Bible?

Catholics are encouraged to study the Bible, so that they understand what it means in their lives. Catholics also use the Bible in prayer. When Catholics go to **Mass**, they hear readings from the Bible and the priest usually teaches about the readings in his sermon. This helps Catholics to hear the meaning of God's word, so that it can help them to follow God's teachings more faithfully.

> **Useful vocabulary**
>
> **revelation:** the way in which God is made known to humans, which Catholics believe is most perfectly done through Jesus
>
> **Bible:** the Christian holy book
>
> **covenant:** an agreement or promise between two or more people; God made covenants with humans such as Abraham and Moses
>
> **Mass:** the central act of worship for Catholics; one of the names for the Sacrament of the Eucharist

Understand

1 What does the word 'revelation' mean for Catholics?

2 Give one example of how humans can know God using reason (our ability to think).

3 Give one example of divine revelation.

4 Why do Catholics call the Bible the 'word of God'?

5 What does the word 'testament' mean?

6 What do the covenants in the Bible reveal about God?

Discern

7 Do you think the order and beauty of the world are evidence of God? If not, how else could they be explained?

8 Give one reason why someone might say that the Bible is the best way for Catholics know God and one reason why someone might disagree with them.

Respond

9 **Either:** Write about a teaching that you already know from the Bible that you think has helped you to know God better.
Or: Write about how you think revelation from God can help a Catholic in their day-to-day life.

HOW SHOULD WE READ THE BIBLE?

Catholics believe that the Bible is the word of God. They believe the Bible is inspired, meaning that the Holy Spirit has guided the authors to write down the truth from God. Catholics believe that the Bible teaches them God's truth, but that they need to interpret the Bible to find this truth. To interpret something means to study it, in order to find its meaning.

The Bible is one book, made up of many books

It's important to recognise that the Bible is a book made up of many books, like a library. Libraries are made up of a variety of books and styles of writing and so is the Bible. There are books that contain poetry, history, letters and words of wisdom, for example. This has an impact on how we read and interpret different teachings from the Bible.

If you think about it, you wouldn't read a poetry book and expect it to give facts about history. You would understand that you are reading someone's carefully chosen words describing something that might be very important to them, or expressing a deep feeling. You would not expect to find dates, locations and facts. This is the same as the Bible. When Catholics read it, they don't think that they are reading a science textbook or a map of the ancient world. They believe it is God's word given to humans to write down.

The Bible is one book, with contributions from many people

Catholics believe that God guided the Bible's writers. There isn't one author, there were many authors behind the Bible. This is really obvious in some places, such as the **Gospels** of Matthew and Mark or the letters of St Paul, because the books are named after their authors. However, even the Gospels are much more complicated than being just one person's view on Jesus – they all draw on different sources of information.

There are also parts of the Bible where it is less obvious who is responsible for each book. The Bible began as a spoken record, kept alive by the first believers, who collected and remembered God's word by sharing it in their communities. This was the usual way of remembering important information at the time. Later, these spoken records were gathered and written down by different people. This explains why sometimes there are different accounts of the same thing – such as the two creation stories.

Useful vocabulary

Gospel: the term Gospel means 'Good News'; the Gospels are the books in the Bible that teach the Good News about Jesus

Link

You will read more about the creation stories (Genesis 1–2) on pages 14–17.

What does this mean for how Catholics read the Bible?

Most Catholics do not read the Bible literally – in other words they do not think that it is word-for-word true. They do believe, however, that it contains great truth, for example revealing God as the almighty creator and everlasting father. The Bible writers used words to do this. However, Catholics believe that God is completely unlike anything or anyone else, so human language can never fully describe God. The **Catechism of the Catholic Church** (CCC) teaches that 'our human words always fall short of the **mystery** of God'.

It can be helpful to consider what the **literary form**, or the style of writing of a particular Bible passage is (for example, history or poetry), and the historical context in which it was written. Understanding the perspective of the Bible's writers can help the reader understand the meaning of the passage they are reading. You might have done the same in English lessons if you've studied the world that the author of a book lived in, so that you can understand their story better. Catholics believe it is important to understand the world that the Bible writers lived in, because it will have shaped how they wrote down the truth about God. By understanding the context and style of writing, Catholics believe that they can understand the **literal sense** of the Bible. This means they can understand what God inspired the writers to communicate.

▲ Catholics believe the Bible contains great truth, for example revealing God as the almighty creator and everlasting father

Understand

1 What does it mean to 'interpret' something?
2 What happened to the spoken information that the earliest followers of God shared within their communities?
3 Why is the role of the human author important for understanding scripture?
4 What is the difference between reading the Bible literally and understanding the literal sense of the Bible?
5 What do Catholics mean when they say the Bible is 'inspired'?

Discern

6 The Catechism says 'our human words always fall short of the mystery of God'. Write down your opinion on this statement giving reasons to back up your point of view.

Respond

7 Has reading pages 12–13 changed how you feel about reading or interpreting the Bible? Explain why.

WHAT DOES GENESIS 1 TEACH ABOUT CREATION?

The first book of the Bible is Genesis. The name Genesis means 'origin', or where something comes from. The first two chapters in Genesis include two **creation** stories. Many Catholics explore these stories to find answers to big questions about the universe and life.

The two creation stories

The two stories in Genesis 1 and 2 give a religious account of how all of creation came to be. Both stories were written by different groups of authors who were inspired by God to answer the big question: where did the world and everything in it, come from? Both stories show the belief that all life comes from God and that God is good, the creator of a good creation.

In Acts of the Apostles, St Paul says '"In him we live and move and have our being"... "For we are indeed his offspring"' (Acts 17:28). This is the heart of the creation stories – Catholics believe that all life comes from God, making every person God's child. Both Genesis creation stories are attempts to talk about where the world and all life came from. The authors knew that their words would never be enough to describe the mystery of God but they wished to share that all life comes from God.

Useful vocabulary

creation: the act of bringing something into existence; or the universe and everything in it (which Catholics believe God created)

Genesis 1:1–2:4

In the first creation story God is presented as creating the universe and everything in it over six days and resting on the seventh. The stages of creation are shown as days. These days are symbolic. They are not 24 hour blocks of time. They show the belief that God created the universe in an organised way, over time.

Day 1
God creates light, separating it from darkness. Light is called 'Day', darkness is called 'Night'.

Day 2
God makes an expanse to separate the waters from each other. God calls the expanse 'Heaven'.

Day 3
God gathers the waters and lets dry land appear, calling it earth. God creates plants and trees.

Day 4
God makes the lights in the sky: sun, moon and stars.

Day 5
God makes living creatures in the waters and the skies.

Day 6
God creates animals that live on the land and then humans.

Day 7
God rests.

Look at the following example from the first day of creation.

> 'And God said, "Let there be light", and there was light. And God saw that the light was good. And God separated the light from the darkness. God called the light Day, and the darkness he called Night. And there was evening and there was morning, the first day.'
>
> *Genesis 1:3–5*

This creation story is written using verses and choruses, like a hymn or a poem for people to share in. At the end of each 'day', there is a set formula of words: 'And there was evening, and there was morning, the [first/second/third, etc.] day.' The story builds up over time so that eventually the world is prepared for humans. When God creates humans, creation is described as 'very good'.

What does this creation story teach about the nature of God?

The opening words of the first creation story are 'In the beginning…' This phrase helps to convey some important beliefs:

- It suggests that God existed before time itself, as an **eternal** being. Creation takes place within space and time, but God is placed outside of creation, making creation occur through a series of instructions. God is shown to be **transcendent**, existing outside of space and time.
- It also suggests that before God began to create, there was nothing except for God. This means that God didn't create from anything that already existed – God's creation came from nothing. This is known as '***creatio ex nihilo***'.

Creatio ex nihilo also shows God to be **omnipotent** (all powerful), since no one else can create from nothing. In this story, when God creates, it is with spoken word rather than materials. At the start of each day, the story reads 'And God said…' and God goes on to say what will be created. This story can help Catholics to realise that God's power is greater than any human power.

Most Catholics don't believe that this story is a literal or factual account of creation. Instead, it helps them to understand what God is like, by showing them how God creates. It expresses to them the value and importance of the world and everything in it.

Useful vocabulary

eternal: exists beyond time and has no beginning or end

transcendent: existing outside of space and time

creatio ex nihilo: the Latin phrase for 'creation out of nothing'

omnipotent: all powerful

Understand

1 In which book of the Bible are the creation stories and what does the name of this book mean?

2 How are the stages of creation shown in the first story in Genesis?

3 Identify two qualities of God seen in the first creation story.

4 What does the first creation story tell us about humans?

5 How does this creation story help Catholics to understand the mystery of who God is?

Discern

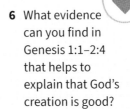

6 What evidence can you find in Genesis 1:1–2:4 that helps to explain that God's creation is good?

7 Do you think that a belief in *creatio ex nihilo* is important? Explain your view.

Respond

8 This is a famous story that describes God right at the beginning of the Bible. It is our introduction to who God is. How would you say God is presented in this story?

WHAT DOES GENESIS 2 TEACH ABOUT CREATION?

We have already read that in Genesis 1 and 2 there are two creation stories. Each is slightly different, but both give Catholics important teachings about God and creation. Catholics believe that God inspired different authors to write accounts of creation, which is why we have two different accounts in Genesis.

Genesis 2:5–25

The second creation story focuses more on the creation of humans. It has a very different style to the first story, because it was written by a different set of authors. Like the first story, it reminds Catholics that all life comes from God. God is shown to create a man first: 'then the LORD God formed the man of dust from the ground and breathed into his nostrils the breath of life, and the man became a living creature' (Genesis 2:7). God places the man in Eden and plants a garden which will provide food and beauty.

God recognises that man needs company and so creates animals:

> " 'Now out of the ground the LORD God had formed every beast of the field and every bird of the heavens and brought them to the man to see what he would call them. And whatever the man called every living creature, that was its name.'
>
> *Genesis 2:19*

▲ *A stained glass window from Our Lady of Victories Church in Kensington, London; it shows the first humans created by God*

God sees that none of the animals is the best helper for man, and so creates a woman from the man's rib. The man sees that she is the right companion for him.

Some people wonder why woman was created from man's rib and why God created her as a 'helper' (Genesis 2:20). Some have taken this to mean that men are more important than women. Others believe that it actually shows how connected all humans are. Woman came from man, who came from God – all life leads back to God and all people are linked to one another.

In this story, God's creation of man is very 'hands on'. God is given physical qualities, such as breathing life into man, to show how close God can be to humans. This is not meant to be interpreted literally. The authors want to show that God was closely involved in creation. This quality of God being close to humans and acting in the world is known as immanence.

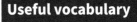

God is shown as **immanent** through the creation of animals, and finally a woman, as companions for the man. God sees the man's loneliness, knows that it isn't good for him to feel alone and responds to this.

Useful vocabulary

immanent: operating in the universe; Catholics believe that God works within the universe to have a relationship with them and to sustain the universe

The creation accounts as symbolic stories

Both creation stories are written to help the reader to understand that God is the creator – this is the literal sense of each story. Both stories rely on symbolism to communicate the belief that God is the creator. This is because humans will never be fully able to find the words to express who God is and because the idea of creating something so enormous as the universe is beyond our understanding. For example, in the first account, written in the structure of a hymn or a poem, God's words are used to create the world. We all know people who can give an order and it happens – such as your teacher telling you to work, and you do. But can you imagine giving an order to create the different parts of the universe? The authors of this story write in a way that readers will be amazed by God's power. In the second account, which reads more like a story, God's closeness to creation is shown when God breathes life into the man and gives man a companion. The authors of this story write in a way so that readers will be moved by God's care and tenderness.

This second account is often seen as a story that shows how God lovingly and carefully made the world as a place for humans to live together. Some Catholics describe this story as symbolic because it paints a picture in our mind which helps us to understand a complicated idea. It doesn't mean that the story is untrue in any way – in fact it teaches some important truths. In this story, God organises the universe, making it calm and full of life.

Understand

1 Give two differences between the creation stories.

2 What do the creation stories literally tell us?

3 What is the literal sense (main point) of the creation stories?

4 What are the different literary forms used in the creation stories?

5 Describe how the authors have helped to show the literal sense of the story to readers.

6 What do we mean when we say the creation accounts are 'symbolic stories'?

Discern

7 Is the image of the first woman (Eve) being made from Adam's rib helpful in thinking about the equality of men and women? Give at least one reason for your answer.

8 'It is important to study both creation stories.' Write a paragraph saying whether you agree or disagree with this statement.

Respond

9 What main messages about human beings does Genesis 2:5–25 give you? Use some examples to back up your answer.

WHAT ARE THE SCIENTIFIC THEORIES ABOUT CREATION?

The creation stories were first shared at a time long before modern scientific explanations of how the universe began. Since the Bible was written, scientists have used the evidence they find in the world to give other answers to the question of where all life came from.

Scientific theories about creation

There are two **scientific theories** that many people accept give us the best explanation of where the world came from and how life came to be as we know it today. These are the **Big Bang theory** and the **theory of evolution**.

The Big Bang theory

This scientific theory gives an explanation of how the universe came to exist. Around 15 billion years ago the universe began with the expansion of a hot, dense point of energy. As the energy cooled, it went through a series of changes, before becoming atoms, which were necessary for the universe and all life to form. Using powerful telescopes, scientists have observed that the universe is still expanding. This provides evidence to support the theory that there was one point from which the universe first began.

The theory of evolution

Charles Darwin's scientific theory suggests that all living things change over many generations to suit their environment, and that this happens because of natural selection (sometimes called 'survival of the fittest'). In his book, *On the Origin of the Species by Means of Natural Selection* (written in 1859) Darwin observed that species evolved to keep features that helped them survive in a particular environment. For example, when he visited the Galapagos Islands, he noted that the finches on each island were slightly different – their beaks had changed over many generations to be more suited to the food found on each island.

ISLAND A   ISLAND B

Responses to these scientific theories

Some atheists (people who do not believe that God exists) would argue that scientific theories such as those about the Big Bang and evolution give the only answer that people need to questions about where the universe and everything in it came from. They would argue that there is plenty of evidence to support these theories and that is why they can be trusted. They might also argue that there is no need for people to read the Bible creation stories any more since science can answer life's big questions.

▲ *Some Christians believe that the accounts of creation in the Bible are literally true; this viewpoint is often called creationism*

The belief that only science can answer all of the big questions about the universe and life is called **scientism**. Many people, religious and non-religious, believe that this is incorrect. They suggest that science can't always tell us the fullest answer.

Some Christians reject the Big Bang theory and the theory of evolution, believing that the Bible accounts of creation are literally true. This viewpoint is often called **creationism**. The Catholic Church rejects creationism because it sees no conflict between the scientific theories about the origins of the universe and the belief in God as creator of everything.

Understand

1 Write a short summary of the Big Bang theory.
2 Write a short summary of the theory of evolution.
3 What might atheists argue about Bible creation stories?
4 What is creationism?

Discern

5 Which do you think give the best explanation of how the universe and life came to be, the Genesis creation stories or the scientific theories about the Big Bang and evolution? Give at least one reason to back up your viewpoint.
6 Give one reason why someone might disagree with you.

Respond

7 Do you think it would make a difference if people only accepted scientific beliefs about the universe and life? Explain your view.

Useful vocabulary

scientific theory: a commonly agreed idea, held by scientists and backed up by evidence

Big Bang theory: the scientific theory that the universe was formed through the expansion of a hot, dense point of energy

theory of evolution: the scientific theory that every living thing changes, over a long period of time, to suit its environment

scientism: the belief that science can provide all of the answers in life

creationism: the belief that the Bible accounts of creation are literally true

OBJECTIVE

In this lesson you will learn about **the Catholic Church's responses to the Big Bang theory and the theory of evolution.**

WHAT DO CATHOLICS BELIEVE ABOUT SCIENTIFIC THEORIES ABOUT CREATION?

Many people think that the evidence used in scientific theories about creation tells them everything they need to know about where the universe and everything in it came from. However, many Catholics believe that science can't answer all of life's big questions and so religious teaching (such as in the creation stories) has a really important role to play in answering them too.

Faith and reason

Catholics believe that **faith** (belief in God) needs to work with **reason** (the ability to use knowledge and intelligence). The scientists who presented the Big Bang theory and the theory of evolution used reason to find evidence to support these theories. This has helped many people to understand the universe and life better. Catholics believe that faith is a gift from God which helps them to understand the world more deeply – and to have the fullest answer to questions about where all life came from.

Catholic responses to creationism and scientism

Most Catholics are not creationists and do not read the creation stories in a literal, word-for-word way. Most Catholics believe that the creation stories show the power, wisdom and goodness of God and that the authors used symbolic language to explain God's qualities to humans.

Catholics also reject scientism because they feel that science can't answer all of the questions that we have about the universe and life. They might say that science can give us some of the answers but that religious teaching helps people to understand the universe and life even more.

Catholic responses to the Big Bang Theory and the theory of evolution

Many Catholics, encouraged by teachings from the Church over time, believe that the Big Bang theory and the theory of evolution are compatible with their faith in God the creator, that is, that they can believe in these theories and in God the creator at the same time.

In 1927, Father (Fr) Georges Lemaître suggested that the universe began from a small 'super atom' and expanded from this point onwards. Lemaître was a Belgian astronomer and cosmologist (a scientist who studies the universe), as well as

Useful vocabulary

faith: personal commitment to God, which includes trusting and obeying God

reason: the ability to think in a clear and logical way

being a Catholic priest. He didn't read the Bible accounts of creation in a literal way and so didn't view the Bible as a scientific account of how the universe and all life was formed. The Bible, for Fr Lemaître, gave essential teaching about how to become closer to God and achieve salvation.

In 1996, Pope St John Paul II taught that it was important for Catholics *not* to think that the theory of evolution was at odds with the Bible, since the Bible creation stories reveal the purpose of humans and the theory of evolution helps people to understand how all life has developed.

In 2014, Pope Francis said that Catholics have to be careful not to read the Bible in a way that makes God seem like 'a magician with a magic wand'. He said that he thought the Big Bang and evolution needed God, since God is the creator of all things. God begins all of creation, and creation develops in a way that God guides.

▲ *Fr Georges Lemaître, scientist and Catholic priest*

What does this mean for Catholics today?

Catholics today are taught by the Pope that there is no conflict between science and religion about creation. This is because the Bible contains faith-based teaching that shows that God made and loves all of creation and gave it all a purpose. Genesis creation stories are not scientific theories. Pope St John Paul II explained that science can explain how human life has evolved but that the Bible reveals its purpose.

It can be argued that God has given humans intelligence and reason so that they can explore and understand the world. Scientists like Lemaître and Darwin used reason to help people understand the world, including how life has become what it is today. However, many Catholics believe that they get the fullest answer to the big questions about life when religion tells them *why* life exists, and science tells them *how*.

Understand

1 Define what Catholics mean by **a)** faith and **b)** reason?
2 Why do most Catholics reject creationism?
3 Why do Catholics reject scientism?
4 What do many Catholics believe about the theories of the Big Bang and evolution?
5 What did Pope St John Paul II say was the difference between the teachings of the Bible and science about how life has evolved?

Discern

6 'If you believe in the Big Bang theory and Darwin's theory of evolution, then the Genesis creation stories can't be true.' Do you agree with this statement? How might a Catholic respond to it?

Respond

7 What big questions do you think the Bible creation stories and the scientific theories about the Big Bang and evolution can answer? Do they help you to understand the world around you?

WHAT MAKES HUMANS DIFFERENT TO THE REST OF CREATION?

OBJECTIVE

In this lesson you will learn about **imago Dei, the idea that humans reflect God's nature.**

When Catholics reflect on God's creation and on human life, they often realise how amazing and beautiful this creation is. This increases their awe and love for God since God has shown power, wisdom and love in this creation.

Humans are created *imago Dei*

> ‘Then God said, "Let us make man in our image, after our likeness. And let them have dominion over the fish of the sea and over the birds of the heavens and over the livestock and over all the earth and over every creeping thing that creeps on the earth."
>
> So, God created man in his own image,
> in the image of God he created him;
> male and female he created them.'

Genesis 1:26–27

Useful vocabulary

imago Dei: a Latin phrase meaning 'in the image of God', the idea that humans reflect God's nature

▲ The Creation of Adam *by Michelangelo, from the ceiling of the Sistine Chapel; this painting shows God giving life to Adam; Adam is shown as a reflection of God, made in God's image*

Imago Dei is a Latin phrase meaning 'image of God'. Catholics believe that humans are made in God's image – this is not about how humans look but rather the way in which they are connected to God as God's children. The belief that humans are created *imago Dei* can help Catholics to understand God a little more since they themselves are a reflection of God. Humans will never have all of God's qualities, or God's perfection, but they can show God's love and make good choices.

Imago Dei means that all humans come from God

The belief that humans are created *imago Dei* is really important since it means that all humans have equal worth. Often in the world, people are divided into different groups – for example male and female, rich and poor – sometimes to make it seem that one group is better than the other. However, Catholics would say that, while every human being is different, all come from God and have equal dignity and worth.

Catholics also believe that all humans are precious to God, who always wants the best for them. Being made in God's image means that humans are God's most special creation. This close connection between God and humans also means that humans can have a relationship with God: God loves them and they can speak to God through their prayers.

Imago Dei means that Catholics have responsibilities to the world and to others

The belief in *imago Dei* is a reminder to Catholics that all people – no matter their age, ability, health, wealth or way of life – are created in God's image. The belief that God has created all people *imago Dei* means that all people need to be treated with dignity and respect.

Many Catholics today give their time and energy to making sure that the world treats all people equally and fairly. For example, CAFOD (the Catholic Agency for Overseas Development) helps communities in the poorest countries gain access to life-changing support, such as education and healthcare.

Being created *imago Dei* means that Catholics believe humans have a God-given sense of right and wrong. This helps Catholics to try to make good choices and to try to stand up to inequality and bring about positive change in the world.

Furthermore, being created *imago Dei* gives humans the responsibility to care for the world, which means taking care of the land, natural resources and all animal life.

Understand

1 Where can Catholics read that humans are created *imago Dei*?

2 What do Catholics mean by 'creation *imago Dei*'?

3 How might a belief in creation *imago Dei* make a Catholic feel close to God?

4 Explain how the belief that humans are created *imago Dei* emphasises that humans have dignity and worth.

5 Write down two ways in which a Catholic could show that they believe that all people are created *imago Dei*.

Discern

6 'Humans are more important than any other part of creation.' Do you agree with this? Write a paragraph to explain your answer.

Respond

7 Consider the world that we live in today. How might the belief that all humans are made *imago Dei* make a positive impact? Try to come up with at least five ideas.

WHAT IS OUR RESPONSIBILITY TO OTHERS?

OBJECTIVE

In this lesson you will think about what **Genesis 1 and 2 teaches Catholics about responsibility to others.**

In the creation stories, God created humans to work together, but we know that this doesn't always happen in the world that we live in. The world is unfair and many people struggle. Many people believe we should help to improve the world we live in. Catholics believe that they have a duty to work to improve the world, so that the goodness that was given by God can be experienced by everyone and so that evil and suffering can be overcome.

Catholic Social Teaching

Catholic Social Teaching is the teaching from the Catholic Church which tries to reduce human suffering caused by injustice and increase cooperation and friendship between all people. The Bible reminds humans that they need to love and respect all people, because all people are created *imago Dei* and are part of one family. Jesus taught through his words and actions that we should always love others, no matter who they are. Catholic Social Teaching uses this teaching in the modern world. The world is always changing and this produces new problems and issues, but the message of God's love stays the same. The Church helps Catholics by showing them how to live in a way that shows God's love to others.

The four core principles of Catholic Social Teaching are: the dignity of the human person, the common good, subsidiarity, and solidarity.

The dignity of the human person

Genesis 1 taught that humans were created in God's image. This means that all people are precious to God, equal in dignity, and worthy of respect. It means that Catholics have a duty to make sure that all people are treated with dignity, no matter who they are. Catholics have a duty to challenge any injustice because they believe that treating others unfairly is not part of God's plan.

Example: The St Vincent de Paul Society run a weekly market in Southend. People pay £3.50 to buy 15 items, which is less than the items are worth. This allows them both the dignity of choice and of contributing to their own welfare.

The common good

In the creation stories, God gives humans all that is needed to be happy and to develop their relationship with God. The common good means that all people should be able to experience the goodness in the world so they can flourish and find happiness in God. Catholics have a duty to make sure that no one is left behind and all people have what they need to develop.

Example: Many Catholics support Mary's Meals which gives children in developing countries free meals at school. This supports their education and helps to break the cycle of poverty. The photo shows volunteers cooking porridge for schoolchildren.

Subsidiarity

The idea of subsidiarity is that higher institutions, such as a country's government, should not take away opportunities for people to be involved in making decisions and bringing about change where they live. It is important for people to have this power since they know best how to change the society that they live in.

Example: CAFOD works in partnership with local communities in developing countries to provide support that the community wants and needs. In Lima, the capital of Peru, CAFOD has worked with an organisation called Warmi Huasi, to help children and young people have a say in decisions that will affect them. In this photo, Micaela (on the left) is talking about the need for safe places for children to play in.

Solidarity

Catholics believe that God created humans as a community to work together. Solidarity means seeing that humans are all members of the same family and depend on one another. Jesus' teaching to 'love your neighbour' is a reminder that all people have a responsibility to each other.

An example: Pax Christi is a Catholic charity which promotes peace and an end to conflict in solidarity with people who suffer as a result of war. The picture on the right shows people at an event called 'No Faith in War', organised by Pax Christi in London in 2019. People gathered to pray and to block road access to trucks delivering weapons to an arms fair.

Catholics believe that Catholic Social Teaching helps them to carry out the duty that God has given humans to care for the world and everything in it. This duty is called **stewardship**. Catholics believe that they are acting as good stewards when they work together to protect people's dignity, making sure that all people have their voices heard, and have a fair share of God's creation.

Useful vocabulary

stewardship: the duty to care for something, in this case, the world and everything in it

Link

Read more about stewardship on page 26.

Understand

1 What do Catholics believe they have a duty to do?
2 What did Jesus teach through his words and actions?
3 What do Catholics believe stays the same, even though the world is changing?
4 What are the four core principles of Catholic Social Teaching?
5 Explain how Catholic Social Teaching helps Catholics to be stewards of God's creation.

Discern

6 'Catholic Social Teaching could change the world.' Write a paragraph explaining your response to this idea.

Respond

7 What can you do to show care for the earth and all creatures living on it? Try to explain one idea.

WHAT IS OUR RESPONSIBILITY TO THE WORLD?

Catholics believe that both of the Genesis creation stories make it clear that humans have a duty to care for the earth. Many people believe we need to care for the world, and everyone and everything in it, not just for the present time but also for all future generations. In recent years, Pope Francis has stressed the importance of this in his encyclical *Laudato si'*.

Stewardship

Stewardship means looking after something. When Catholics talk about stewardship of creation, this means the duty that God has given to humans to care for the created world, and everything in it.

This responsibility is written about in both creation stories.

> " 'And God said to them, "Be fruitful and multiply and fill the earth and subdue it, and have dominion over the fish of the sea and over the birds of the heavens and over every living thing that moves on the earth."'
>
> *Genesis 1:28*

Humans are given great power and responsibility. However, they should not misuse this and should instead show the same care for the world as God has done. God has made a good creation and has given humans the responsibility to act with goodness, in order that the world and everything in it can remain good.

In the second creation story, man is put into the garden 'to work it and keep it' (Genesis 2:15). This shows that God trusted humans to care for his creation. Furthermore, God gives Adam the responsibility of naming the creatures:

> " 'Now out of the ground the LORD God formed every beast of the field and every bird of the heavens, and brought them to the man to see what he would call them. And whatever the man called every living creature, that was its name.'
>
> *Genesis 2:19*

God uses his power to create the animals and Adam uses his God-given creativity to name them. The story shows that humans are made to work with God and that the responsibility that God gives to humans will have lasting impact. In the story, the names that Adam gave were the names that the animals became known by.

Laudato si'

In 2015, Pope Francis wrote a letter to the whole world called *Laudato si': On care for our common home*. *Laudato si'* is a medieval Italian phrase meaning 'Praise be to you' – the words of a prayer by St Francis who gave praise to God for the world, which is God's gift and our common home. 'Our common home' is another name for the earth – we all live on the earth and share the earth's resources, so all people need to care for it, not just for today but for future generations.

Pope Francis explains that the Genesis creation stories show that human life is centred on relationships 'with God, with our neighbour and with the earth itself' (*Laudato si'* 66). He says that humans have misunderstood God's instructions and instead of caring for the earth, they have misused their authority and caused harm.

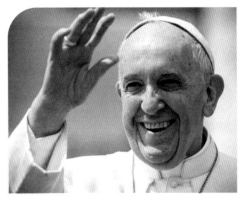

▲ *Pope Francis*

However, God continues to love and care for humans, giving them the chance to be forgiven for their **sins** and have a good relationship with God, others and the world again.

Useful vocabulary

sin: to go against God's law

Responding to 'the cry of the earth and the cry of the poor'

Pope Francis says that stewardship is responding to 'the cry of the earth and the cry of the poor' (*Laudato si'* 49). The Pope encourages all people to stop harming the world and to try to save it, for example, by using natural resources such as water more wisely and taking action to address the problem of climate change.

'The cry of the earth and the cry of the poor' is also about those living in poverty in the world who are often ignored and who suffer the most. He says that environmental damage harms people living in poverty more than anyone else. In *Laudato si'*, Pope Francis describes humans as 'brothers and sisters', which links to the first teaching in Genesis 1: that humans are made in God's image, all equal and connected, with the same father – God. Everyone has a responsibility to help those living in poverty and to stop the environmental damage that harms less-developed countries more than wealthy countries.

Understand

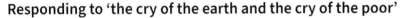

1. What do Catholics mean by 'stewardship'?
2. What is the name of the letter that Pope Francis wrote to the world about stewardship?
3. What does it mean to call the earth 'our common home'?
4. What does the idea of stewardship mean for how Catholics should act? In your answer make reference to **a)** the second creation story in Genesis **b)** Pope Francis' letter *Laudato si'* **c)** the four core principles of Catholic Social Teaching (see pages 24–25).

Discern

5. Do you think it's more important to care for the world or to care for other people? Or, are both important? Give at least two reasons for your opinion.

Respond

6. Catholics believe that the world is made by God and that humans have a responsibility for it. Do you agree with this belief, or with part of of it? How do your beliefs influence how you treat the world and other people?

WHAT IS THE ROLE OF PRAYER?

Prayer is the way in which people communicate with God. Religious believers pray in different ways, but all pray so that they can become closer to God.

Prayer is a part of many different faiths

Religious people from many faiths communicate with God through prayer. Prayer is an important aspect of having a religious faith. Many religious believers see it as important to spend time with God to get to know God and feel God's presence in their lives. There are differences in how people of different faiths pray, for example Muslims pray five times a day, at particular times, and many Hindus have special places in their homes that are the focus of their prayers, called shrines. However, all religious people share the same belief that prayer brings them closer to God in their lives.

▲ *Many Hindus set up spaces in their homes as a focus for their prayer, called shrines*

Prayer is a response to revelation

Often people compare prayer to a conversation. When we are in a conversation, we respond to someone else. Prayer is the response to God's revelation. When a person becomes aware of the existence of God and who God is, they often respond through prayer – they talk to God and share their lives with God.

The prayer might be to thank and praise God for the beautiful world that God created or to thank God for working in someone's life.

Prayer is a response to the call to covenant

The Bible shows that people such as Abraham and Moses entered covenants with God. These were promises or agreements that strengthened the relationship between humans and God. These covenants expressed how much God loved the human race and encouraged people to live in the way that God called them to. Catholics believe that when they pray, they are placing their trust in God, just as Abraham and Moses did in their covenants with God. These covenants didn't end

Useful vocabulary

prayer: the way in which humans communicate with God

Link

Go to pages 10–11 to read more about revelation and covenant.

with Abraham and Moses – all people are called to be in a relationship with God and Catholics believe that this was made possible through Jesus' sacrifice when he was crucified.

What does the Catholic Church teach about prayer?

The Catholic Church defines prayer as 'the raising of our hearts and minds to God' (CCC 2559). This quotation means that prayer is an action of giving yourself completely to God. When many Catholics pray, they try to focus completely on God, with their heart and with their mind. This shows the Catholic belief that people should love God more than anything else and so when Catholics pray, they place God first and try to think only of God.

Catholics believe that God is beyond what humans can understand. However, they believe that prayer helps them to walk with God, so by continuing to communicate with God through prayer, they build up a stronger and closer relationship with God. Jesus encouraged this close relationship when he taught the disciples how to pray, telling them that God should be called 'Our Father'.

On page 27 we found out that the title of Pope Francis' letter, *Laudato si'*, means 'Praise be to you' – a reminder that Catholics are called to thank and praise God for the beautiful creation of the earth, as well as act as stewards of creation. Humans are unlike any other created beings because they are created *imago Dei*, meaning that they can pray and have a relationship with God since they are made by God and reflect God.

▲ *A woman praying in a church*

Understand

1 Why do people from many different religions pray?

2 What is prayer a response to?

3 How is prayer like entering into a covenant with God?

4 How does the Catholic Church define prayer?

5 Explain what the phrase *Laudato si'* means to Catholics.

6 Give two reasons why Catholics might say that prayer is an important part of their life.

Discern

7 Do you think prayer is the best way to show faith in God? Give a reason for your opinion.

Respond

8 What does prayer mean to you, in your life?

WHAT CAN WE DO TO PROTECT CREATION?

OBJECTIVE

In this lesson you will learn about **how humans can help to care for the created world.**

Many people, from all over the world, believe it is important to care for the environment for different reasons. This is particularly important for Catholics since it is part of their duty as stewards of creation and a key part of Catholic Social Teaching. One major goal in this effort to care for the world is **sustainable development**.

What is sustainable development?

In both Genesis creation stories, God gives responsibility to humans to care for the earth. This is not just a message for the earliest people who followed God – this is a message that Catholics believe is essential today.

To sustain something means to keep it going. When we talk about sustainability, we are talking about how to live in a way that prevents harm to the environment and prevents the earth's resources running out. If a new housing development is being planned, it's important to think about how to prevent damage to the eco-system, and the impact on local wildlife.

When decisions about sustainability are made, they fall into three categories:
- **Environmental** – how to care for the created world now and in the future
- **Economic** – how to make sure that people are able to afford to live
- **Social** – how to enjoy living with the people around you

Often, it is people who are in poverty who suffer the most as a result of environmental, economic or social problems. Pope Francis calls people to respond to 'the cry of the earth and the cry of the poor' (*Laudato si'* 49), and many Catholics feel it is a duty from God to care for the world and to consider the needs of those who are experiencing poverty first.

> **Useful vocabulary**
>
> **sustainable development:** carefully managing the use of the earth's resources so that they are not destroyed or used up as a result of human activities

> **Link**
>
> Read more about Pope Francis' call to action in *Laudato si'* on page 27.

Some examples of sustainable work

In 2015, the United Nations (UN) developed 17 Sustainable Development Goals. They are:

1 No poverty	**8** Decent work and economic growth	**13** Climate action
2 Zero hunger	**9** Build industry, innovation and infrastructure	**14** Conserve and protect life below water
3 Good health and well-being	**10** Reduce inequalities	**15** Conserve and protect life on land
4 Quality education		
5 Gender equality	**11** Sustainable cities and communities	**16** Peace, justice and strong institutions
6 Clean water and sanitation	**12** Responsible consumption and production	
7 Affordable and clean energy		**17** Partnerships for the goals

These goals are a call to action to end suffering and poverty, and to care for the world and all people so that by 2030 the world is a fairer and safer place.

CAFOD (the Catholic Agency for Overseas Development) works on many projects that support sustainable development in cities and communities, which is number 11 on the UN's 17 Sustainable Development Goals list. Here is one case study from Bangladesh:

Eco-villages

In southern Bangladesh, CAFOD is working with the Bangladesh Association for Sustainable Development (BASD) to establish 24 'eco-villages' – where all villagers are supported to ensure their farming is sustainable.

The area is threatened by cyclones, rising sea levels and salty soil, making it challenging to grow food. BASD provide training in eco-friendly methods of farming, like making organic pesticides and fertilisers, growing crops in raised beds, and planting protective tree barriers. Those who have participated in the training go on to share their knowledge with their neighbours and children. As a result, the village roofs and gardens are covered with flourishing mangoes, coconuts and aubergines.

12-year-old Dristy describes her eco-village as a green and quiet place with clean air where lots of fruit and vegetables grow. She has taught her friends how to plant trees organically. Dristy says: 'I would like to tell people my age in other countries that they too should plant trees in their gardens, and they should use organic fertiliser instead of chemicals, which are bad for the soil and the environment. I think we can learn from each other.'

▲ *Dristy wants to encourage others to grow crops in a sustainable way*

Understand

1 What responsibility did God give to humans in both creation stories?

2 What does 'sustainability of creation' mean?

3 What are the three categories of sustainability?

4 Using the Genesis creation stories and *Laudato si',* explain why Catholics feel they should care for the environment and all humans on the earth.

5 What is the aim of the UN's 17 Sustainable Development Goals?

Discern

6 'Sustainability is something that everyone should focus on.' Give one reason to agree with this statement and one to disagree.

Respond

7 What can you do to care for the earth and for other people? Try to identify at least three ideas.

CAN ART HELP CATHOLICS UNDERSTAND CREATION?

Art is often used in Christianity to communicate beliefs and teachings because it can be a helpful way of expressing complicated ideas. Colours, images and symbols can help people to explore and understand beliefs and teachings and feel closer to God.

Genesis Frontispiece: Creation (Genesis 1:1–2:3)

The piece of art on this page is Donald Jackson's *Genesis Frontispiece: Creation (Genesis 1:1–2:3)*. It is from the St John's Bible, which is a completely handwritten and illustrated Bible. Donald Jackson is an English calligrapher (an artist who specialises in beautiful handwriting), who was asked in 1998 by the monks at St John's Abbey in Minnesota to lead in making the first handwritten and illustrated copy of the Bible for over five hundred years. The monks saw the project as a way to share the story of the Bible and inspire people in the modern world.

How does this artwork show the creation story?

A frontispiece is an illustration facing the front page of a book, meaning that this image will be the first illustration a person sees when they open the St John's Bible. There are a number of different elements to this piece of art.

Firstly, you will notice that there are seven vertical columns. Each of these reflect the days of creation in the first Genesis creation story. Over the top of the image is a raven. The raven symbolises prophecy – God's communication to the world. It is a reminder that Genesis shows creator God to be a God who speaks and is involved with creation,

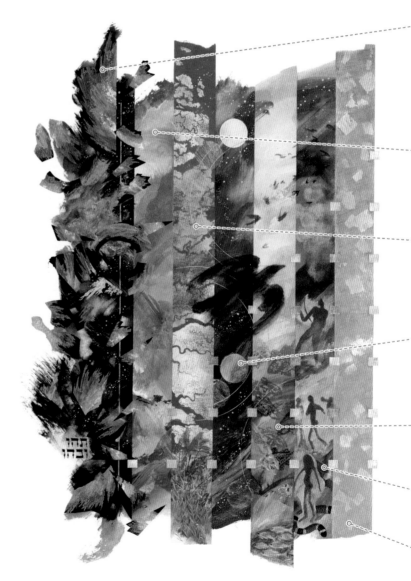

▲ Genesis Frontispiece: Creation (Genesis 1:1–2:3) *by Donald Jackson*

rather than being separate from the world. The blocks of gold show the movement of the seven days of creation, as they count down to the day of rest.

Link

Read more about the first Genesis creation story on pages 14–15.

Day 1: The fragments and shapes at the beginning are chaotic. The Hebrew words on the bottom left mean 'chaos'. Genesis 1:2 says: 'The earth was without form and void, and darkness was over the face of the deep. And the Spirit of God was hovering over the face of the waters.' To the right of the first day there is a gold line which represents the moment God says 'Let there be light' (Genesis 1:3).

Day 2: The swirling blues and greys in this image show that on day two God separated the waters on the earth from the waters above the earth by putting the heavens or the sky between them.

Day 3: This panel shows satellite images from the Nile Delta. In Genesis 1:9 God commands that the land be separated from the seas.

Day 4: The solar system is shown – the Bible says that God created lights in the heavens to be signs for seasons and to give light to the earth.

Day 5: On day five, the Bible says that God created the creatures in the sky and in the waters. This panel shows birds in the lighter blue section above and fish, including images of fish fossils, in the aquamarine section below.

Day 6: Prehistoric rock paintings are used to show that on this day God created humans.

Day 7: On this day, the Bible teaches that God rested and so gold is used to shown that God is resting and contemplating creation.

A comparison with *The Creation of Adam*

On page 22 you can see *The Creation of Adam* by Michaelangelo. This is a famous piece of art which focuses on God's creation of Adam. This artwork reflects Catholic beliefs that God created humans *imago Dei*, because Adam reflects God. God is shown to be above the earth and at a distance from Adam. This presents God as transcendent (outside of space and time). God is shown with a strong body, suggesting omnipotence, and is older, suggesting that God is eternal. This artwork is an interesting contrast to *Genesis Frontispiece: Creation (Genesis 1:1–2:3)* since it focuses much more closely on the creation of humans, much like the second Genesis creation story.

Understand

1 Why do Christians create religious art?
2 Why did the monks of St John's Abbey want to produce this new copy of the Bible?
3 What is the meaning of the raven in this piece of art?
4 Which account of creation does *Genesis Frontispiece: Creation* show?

Discern

5 Explain how Donald Jackson showed the Genesis creation story in *Genesis Frontispiece: Creation*.
6 Look at *The Creation of Adam* on page 22. What ideas about God and creation do you think the artist, Michaelangelo, was trying to show? Compare and contrast this picture with Donald Jackson's *Genesis Frontispiece*.
7 Which of these two artworks do you think best represent Catholic beliefs about creation? Explain your answer.

Respond

8 Has what you have learned from looking closely at these artworks made you think differently about the world around you?

WHAT CAN WE LEARN FROM SISTER DOROTHY STANG?

OBJECTIVES

In this lesson you will learn about **Sr Dorothy Stang's life and how she worked to help protect the Amazon rainforest.**

Catholics believe everyone has a responsibility to care for the environment. Some people put this responsibility at the centre of their lives, dedicating their life and work to protecting the earth. We have learned that in the Genesis creation stories, God gave the duty of stewardship to all people. Pope Francis asked Catholics to respond to the 'cry of the earth and the cry of the poor'. Sister (Sr) Dorothy Stang did this in her work to help protect the Amazon rainforest and support the people who depend on it.

Who was Sr Dorothy Stang?

Sr Dorothy Stang was born in America in 1931. She became a nun and worked as a schoolteacher for many years. In 1966 Sr Dorothy moved to Brazil. Part of her mission was to share the Gospel and help build Christian communities. Within these communities, Sr Dorothy helped to support settler farmers who had been given land in the area so they could make a living. She was passionate about protecting the rainforest, so she helped bring the farmers together to give them greater power in challenging deforestation (the cutting down of large areas of the rainforest). Sr Dorothy's faith in God motivated her to spend the rest of her life doing this work in Brazil. On 12 February 2005 Sr Dorothy was murdered. Her killers had been hired by two wealthy landowners who wanted to stop her campaigns to save the rainforest. Many people call Sr Dorothy a **martyr**, meaning that she died for her faith.

▲ *Sr Dorothy Stang often wore a t-shirt with the words 'The death of the forest is the end of our lives' printed on it.*

Protecting the rainforest

Sr Dorothy Stang made stewardship of the earth her life's work. She is best known for her work to help protect the Amazon rainforest. Rainforests are vital to the health of the whole world. Many people call rainforests 'the lungs of the earth' since they absorb carbon dioxide and release oxygen, which can help to stabilize the climate. Rainforests also add water to the atmosphere, which falls as rain, feeding rivers and lakes, and watering crops. Rainforests are an important home to many species of animals and plants and are a source of food and medicines. The rainforest is also home to many Indigenous peoples (the first people to have lived there).

Useful vocabulary

martyr: someone who dies for their faith

However, the rainforests are continually under threat since they are large expanses of land which some people think would be better used for grazing animals and growing foods. Eighty per cent of the deforestation of the Amazon rainforest has been for grazing cattle to support the beef and leather industries. Another cause of deforestation is logging (cutting down trees to use or sell the wood). When trees are destroyed, the carbon dioxide they had been storing is released, which adds to the problem of climate change. Deforestation also leads to droughts in the local area. When the land is destroyed, many Indigenous peoples lose their homes and ways of life.

Sr Dorothy knew how much the world depends on rainforests and wanted to stop deforestation. Though she saw God's creation being destroyed she worked tirelessly to protect it.

Supporting sustainability

When we treat people with respect and care, we treat them with dignity. Throughout her whole life, Sr Dorothy showed the importance of human dignity. She worked with small communities of settler farmers who were under pressure from ranchers and loggers who wanted to take their land, threatening their homes and livelihoods. These farmers worked on small plots of land, using farming methods that didn't harm the rainforest. Sr Dorothy worked to support their way of life. She did this in many ways, for example through education. She set up 26 schools to educate the next generations of farmers, and she developed a fruit co-operative so that families could sell the produce they grew. Her goal was to strengthen the farming communities and to bring them greater power in the face of such pressure.

Sr Dorothy knew that her life was in danger – lots of people wanted to stop her work because they saw her as a threat to their businesses and wealth. However, she did not stop, even saying that she was prepared to suffer and die rather than see this unfair treatment of people continue. Following her murder, the Catholic Church recognised Sr Dorothy as a martyr and Brazilian President Luiz Inácio Lula da Silva put a large amount of land in the area that Sr Dorothy had worked under environmental protection.

▲ *The Amazon rainforest occupies around 6 million square kilometres*

Understand

1 Identify three things that Sr Dorothy did in Brazil.
2 Why was Sr Dorothy killed?
3 Why is the rainforest so important?
4 How did Sr Dorothy show care for the earth and care for other humans?
5 What did President Luiz Inácio Lula da Silva do that showed the impact of Sr Dorothy's work?

Discern

6 How important do you think Catholic beliefs about stewardship and human dignity were in Sr Dorothy Stang's work?
7 'Everyone should follow Sr Dorothy's example.' Do you agree with this quotation? Write a paragraph to back up your opinion.

Respond

8 Do you find Sr Dorothy inspiring? Explain your response.

ASSESSMENT

Key vocabulary

Write a definition for these key terms.

God	revelation	literal sense	literary form
creation	creationism	scientism	prayer
stewardship			

Knowledge check

1 Which of these phrases is the meaning of stewardship?

   a To care for and protect something.

   b To do what we like with something we've been given.

   c To care for and protect our own belongings.

2 Copy out and complete the following sentence:

   CAFOD stands for Catholic Agency F................ O................ D................

3 Copy out and correct this sentence: Pope Francis says we should respond to the cry of the animals and the cry of the rich.

4 How many accounts of creation are there in the book of Genesis?

5 What is the literal translation of 'imago Dei'?

6 In 2015, Pope Francis wrote a letter about stewardship. What is it called?

7 What is revelation?

8 Describe Catholic beliefs about prayer.

9 The creation stories in Genesis are sometimes called 'symbolic stories'. Describe what is meant by this.

10 Explain the difference between a creationist and a scientistic explanation of how the universe began.

TIP

Try to define a 'symbolic story' and try to include at least one example of something from the creation stories that could be understood as symbolic.

TIP

Before you start, make sure you are clear what is meant by a 'creationist' and 'scientistic' view. The question isn't asking which you think is correct – but rather can you name one key difference between them?

Extended writing activity

This assessment is for you to show what you have learned in this chapter and to develop your extended writing skills. Here is a big question:

What do the creation stories teach us about God and humans?

This can be broken down into two smaller questions. Your teacher will direct you to which questions they want you to answer.

1   Let's think about the first part of the big question. Start with a paragraph to answer the question **'What do the creation stories teach us about God?'**

You could use 'Point-Evidence-Explain' to write at least one paragraph to answer this question.

Point – make the point for your paragraph

Evidence – give evidence to back up your point

Explain – what the evidence means and how it answers the question

Here's an example:

The Genesis creation stories teach that God is omnipotent, meaning all ○
powerful. In Genesis 1, God creates by speaking – for example, saying ○
'Let there be light.' When God speaks about something to be created, it is
created. No one else can create like that and so the creation stories ○
show that God's power makes God unlike anyone or anything else.

Try to write at least one more paragraph about God. Below are some sentence starters and a list of ideas about what the point of your paragraph(s) could be.

Genesis 1/Genesis 2/the creation stories show that God is...

The evidence for this is...

This means that...

> **Words you could use:**
>
> all loving
> transcendent (beyond space and time)
> immanent (experienced in the world)
> eternal (has always existed and always will)

2   For the second part of the big question, write some paragraphs to answer the question **'What do the creation stories teach us about humans?'** You can use the same 'Point-Evidence-Explain' approach for this. **Try to write two or more paragraphs on this.**

> **Words you could use:**
>
> imago Dei (made in God's image)
> stewards of creation
> in relationship with others

TIP

- *Remember that there are two creation stories. You don't have to write about them separately, but you should choose information from both to use in your answer.*

- *Really good answers will include specific information from the creation stories, specialist vocabulary and evidence that you understand this information yourself.*

1   In this first sentence, the **point** for the paragraph is given: God is omnipotent.

2   In this second sentence, specific **evidence** from Genesis 1 has been given to back up the point made – God creates by spoken word.

3   In these the last two sentences, there is an **explanation** of the point, which shows the student's personal understanding and helps to answer the question.

PROPHECY AND PROMISE

Introduction

The Bible has been important to many people throughout history and has shaped people's views on how to treat others and care for the world. Why is it such an important book to so many people?

Catholics, like all Christians, believe that the Bible is a record of God's revelation to human beings. **Throughout the Old and New Testaments, God reveals himself** in different ways, such as through the prophets, in laws and fully in the person of Jesus.

In this chapter we are going to consider why the Bible, also known as *scripture*, is an authoritative (or trusted) text. We will explore how the Bible is a library of books with many different authors and literary forms. However, **Catholics believe that all of the Bible's authors were inspired by God,** through the Holy Spirit. **Catholics believe that the Bible is without error and contains the information that guides humans to salvation.** Many books of the Old Testament come from the Hebrew scriptures, and we will explore their importance in the Jewish faith, and how they are relevant for Catholics today.

Catholics believe that God is revealed fully in Jesus Christ and that Jesus can be known through the tradition of the Church (for example, the teachings of the Church and the writings of saints) and the scriptures that record his life, ministry, death and resurrection. Both tradition and scripture have to be interpreted by the authority of the Church, through the authority of the Pope and bishops to teach, which is called the magisterium.

Scripture is central to the life and practice of the Catholic faith. It is used in Mass and to inspire prayer, for example the Rosary is a unique way for Catholics to meditate on the events of Jesus' life. We will look at one example of a beautiful artistic presentation of scripture, designed to reflect its meaning and importance. Finally, we will look at how the language of the Bible has made an impact on our everyday use of language. This is an example of how **scripture, which is at the very heart of the Catholic faith, has also had a wider influence on how we live today**.

HOW DO YOU NAVIGATE THE BIBLE?

OBJECTIVE

In this lesson you will learn **how to find a Bible reference.**

Christians believe that the Bible is very important as it contains the teachings of God and the life and **ministry** of Jesus – and these influence how Christians live their lives. As we learned in Chapter 1, the Bible is like a library: it contains many different smaller books within itself. This means that Christians navigate the Bible differently from other books, so that they can find the teaching that they need. When Christians use the word 'scripture', they are referring to the Bible.

Where is the Old Testament in the Bible?

The **Old Testament** is found at the beginning of the Bible. It begins with the creation of the world in Genesis and the start of God's relationship with humanity. It then goes on to show the history of God's relationship with the Jewish people and how God built this relationship with covenants, laws, promises and **prophecies**.

In Catholic Bibles, the Old Testament contains 46 books.

Link

Read more about covenants on pages 10–11.

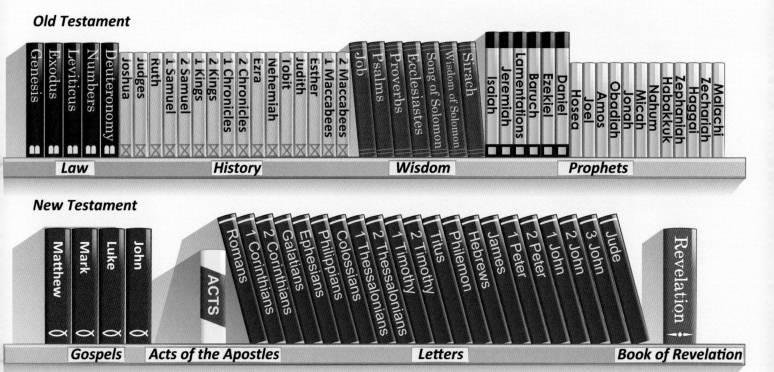

Old Testament

Genesis · Exodus · Leviticus · Numbers · Deuteronomy | Joshua · Judges · Ruth · 1 Samuel · 2 Samuel · 1 Kings · 2 Kings · 1 Chronicles · 2 Chronicles · Ezra · Nehemiah · Tobit · Judith · Esther · 1 Maccabees · 2 Maccabees | Job · Psalms · Proverbs · Ecclesiastes · Song of Solomon · Wisdom of Solomon · Sirach | Isaiah · Jeremiah · Lamentations · Baruch · Ezekiel · Daniel · Hosea · Joel · Amos · Obadiah · Jonah · Micah · Nahum · Habakkuk · Zephaniah · Haggai · Zechariah · Malachi

Law   **History**   **Wisdom**   **Prophets**

New Testament

Matthew · Mark · Luke · John | Acts | Romans · 1 Corinthians · 2 Corinthians · Galatians · Ephesians · Philippians · Colossians · 1 Thessalonians · 2 Thessalonians · 1 Timothy · 2 Timothy · Titus · Philemon · Hebrews · James · 1 Peter · 2 Peter · 1 John · 2 John · 3 John · Jude | Revelation

Gospels   **Acts of the Apostles**   **Letters**   **Book of Revelation**

▲ *The 73 books of the Bible are arranged into groups, which helps Catholics to find the books they are looking for*

Where is the New Testament in the Bible?

The **New Testament** is found in the second half of the Bible. It is the fulfilment of the prophecies and hopes found in the Old Testament and tells the story of the New Covenant that God made with humans through Jesus, the Son of God. The New Testament shows the life, ministry, death and resurrection of Jesus, from the perspective of four different Gospel writers. It also shows how the early Church began to grow in the Acts of the Apostles and through the letters sent by early Church leaders (especially St Paul) to different Christian communities.

The New Testament is made up of 27 books.

How to find passages in scripture using Bible references

Most Catholics do not tend to read the Bible from cover to cover, but look up specific passages which are relevant to what they need. To help find passages easily, we use references to the **book**, **chapter** and **verse** of the Bible, as shown below.

This refers to the **book** of the Bible where the passage can be found. You can use the contents page at the front of the book to locate it. This is the Gospel of Luke, from the New Testament.

Luke 1 : 5–25

The first number of the reference always refers to the **chapter** that this piece of scripture is found in. Each book of the Bible has large numbers to indicate the start of each chapter, so when looking in the Gospel of Luke you would firstly search for a large number 1 to find the correct chapter.

The second number(s) after the colon (:) indicate the **verse**(s) where the passage is found. Every chapter is divided into small pieces called verses. In the Bible, verses are indicated with numbers much smaller than the chapter numbers. After finding chapter 1 in Luke's Gospel, you would search within this chapter for the small number 5. As this passage is Luke 1:5–25, you would read from verse 5 up to and including verse 25.

Useful vocabulary

ministry: the work Jesus carried out to spread the word of God in the three years between his baptism and crucifixion

scripture: the holy book(s) of a religion; in Christianity it is the Bible

Old Testament: the books of the first half of the Bible showing the creation of the world and God's relationship with the Jewish people

prophecies: God's messages for the world, warnings, encouragements or predictions

New Testament: the books of the second half of the Bible, which tell the story of Jesus' life, ministry, death and resurrection, and the establishment of the early Church

Link

Read more about the books in the Bible on pages 11–13 and 44–45.

Understand

1 Why can the Bible be described as a 'library'?

2 What is the main theme of the New Testament?

3 What three things make up a Bible reference?

4 Look up *Luke 10:9* and *2 Samuel 7:4*. What are the first words of these passages?

Discern

5 'It is easy to navigate the Bible.' Give one reason to agree with this statement and one reason to disagree.

Respond

6 Has reading how to navigate the Bible made you more confident in using the Bible? Explain your answer.

WHY IS THE BIBLE READ IN TRANSLATION?

OBJECTIVE

*In this lesson you will explore **why the Bible is read in translation.***

As we know, the Bible is made up of many smaller books. These books were written thousands of years ago and originate from many different places; they were not written in English. The Bible took centuries to be compiled and translated (changed into another language) into the version we read today. This means that most Christians do not read the Bible in its original language.

The original languages of the Bible

There are three biblical languages: **Hebrew, Aramaic and Greek**. The Old Testament is a collection of writings that were first written by Jewish people thousands of years ago. It is mainly written in biblical Hebrew but has some small sections written in Aramaic. The Old Testament shows the beginning of God's relationships with all of humanity, particularly with the Jewish people.

At the time when the New Testament was being written, the Roman empire had conquered Greece. As a result of this, Greek culture and language spread throughout the empire, with many people speaking *koine* Greek (common Greek) as their preferred language. The New Testament, therefore, was written in *koine* Greek. As this could be understood by many people, this helped to spread the teachings of the New Testament throughout the Greek-speaking world.

Why was the Bible translated many times?

Over the years, the Bible has been translated into different languages so that it could be read and understood by more people. Around the third century BC the Old Testament was translated into Greek so that people from Greek-speaking Jewish communities could read it. In the third century AD, St Jerome, a Catholic scholar, began translating the Bible into Latin, with the aim of having one common text which would be used throughout the Catholic Church. This became known as the Vulgate. In the fifteenth and sixteenth centuries many new translations of the Bible were published for ordinary people to read, including a German translation and an English translation.

Useful vocabulary

Hebrew, Aramaic and Greek: languages spoken in the area where Jesus grew up; some books of the Bible were written in these languages

Link

Most of the texts in the Old Testament are also in the Tanakh, or Jewish Bible. Read more about the connection between these books on pages 46–47.

▲ *This extract from the Bible is in Hebrew*

The Bible is the most translated book in the world. It is read in translation because most people cannot understand Hebrew, Aramaic, or Greek. When you read the Bible, you are reading the words in the way that the translator understood them. It can be difficult to translate some words and phrases exactly. Some translations try to keep the original grammar and word order, which makes them hard to read. Other translations try to follow the meaning, rather than keep the exact words, and can be much easier for most people to understand. The Catholic Church has approved particular translations of the Bible, which give confidence to the reader that the message is accurate and authentic.

There are many different English translations of the Bible

For many years the only language the Bible was available in was Latin. The Bible was first translated into English in the 1300s. Then, in the 1500s, William Tyndale's English translation became a model for later translations. The most significant event was the publishing of the King James Bible in 1611, which became the official English Bible of the **Protestant** Church. Since then, there have been different versions of the Bible published under different names, which all have the King James version as their source. Many have tried to update the language used or remove inaccuracies from previous translations.

The way that the Bible has been translated depends on the understanding and logic of the person doing the translating. This means that there can be many different translations of the same verse, each with a slightly different wording. The way a Bible verse is translated can have a big impact on how that verse is understood, as the translation can influence how a person reads it. For example, some English translations of the Old Testament translate the Hebrew word 'Sheol' to the English word 'Hell'. However, when the Old Testament was being written, the idea of hell as we know it today did not exist. Hell is most of often understood as a fiery place of punishment for the wicked, who live eternally without God. Sheol, however, is thought of as a dark place deep down in the earth – a place for the dead. This shows how a different translation of even just a single word can completely change how a passage is understood.

Different Bibles are used by different Christian groups, and not all Bibles include all the same content. For example, the Catholic version of the Bible has 73 books in total, whereas most Protestant versions only have 66 books.

Useful vocabulary

Protestant: Christians who belong to any Church branch that protested against and separated from the Catholic Church following the Reformation in the sixteenth century

Understand

1 What does it mean to say that the Bible is 'read in translation'?
2 Name the original three languages of the Bible.
3 Give two reasons why there are many different English translations of the Bible.
4 How might the way that a Bible passage has been translated impact a reader's understanding of it? Give an example to support your point.

Discern

5 Do you think it is important to recognise that the Bible is a translated text? Give reasons for your opinion.

Respond

6 Explain why translation of the Bible has helped it to remain an important text over thousands of years.

HOW IS THE BIBLE A LIBRARY OF BOOKS?

The Bible is one way in which God communicates and gives humans important information. It was written by human authors who were **inspired** by God to write what was revealed to them and what they witnessed. Each book of the Bible is unique, with a different message, aim and **literary form**.

The Bible is a library of books

The Greek word *biblia* means 'book' and is the root of the word 'bible'. Within the Bible is a whole library of books that were written over a period of around 1,500 years. Many sacred writings were compiled during the early years of the Church, and it took many years for the books of the Bible to be confirmed. The agreed list of books that are included in the Bible is called the **canon of scripture**. These books were confirmed at some point in the first centuries of the Church. They are shown in the correct order in the bookshelf artwork on page 40, beginning with Genesis and ending with Revelation.

To understand the Bible, we need to understand each book separately and then understand how each fits into the whole Bible. Reading the Bible from start to finish is not necessarily the best way to understand it.

There are different human authors of the Bible

The Bible has around 40 different authors, each with their own unique background and style of writing. But, if the books were written by 40 different human authors, how can it be said that the Bible is the word of God? ***Dei Verbum*** ('Word of God'), a key Catholic document, answers this question:

> **"** 'For **Sacred Scripture** is the **word of God** inasmuch as it is consigned to **writing under the inspiration** of the divine **Spirit**.'
>
> *Dei Verbum 9*

This means the Bible is the word of God because the people who wrote it were guided to know what to write by the **Holy Spirit**. God's word flowed into the authors: their words were from God and this gives the Bible authority.

Useful vocabulary

inspired: 'God breathed'; the belief that the Holy Spirit guides a person to act or write what is good and true

literary form the style of writing used, for example a letter or a poem

canon of scripture: the agreed list of books that make up the Catholic Bible

Dei Verbum: the Latin phrase for 'Word of God'; also a document from the Second Vatican Council explaining how Jesus is the Word of God

Holy Spirit: the third person of God and the Trinity, who Christians believe inspires people

▲ *Within the Bible is a whole library of books that were written over a period of around 1,500 years*

Understanding the literary forms of scripture is important

The authors of the Bible came from different times and cultures, and each person wrote with different intentions and in different literary forms. The table below shows one way these forms can be divided.

Old Testament	**Law**	The five books of Moses (Pentateuch). They offer guidance on how to live and worship God.
	History	These books explain the relationship that God has with the Jewish people and their history.
	Wisdom	These books offer advice on how to be a good person and how to maintain a close relationship with God. They include songs, poetry and sayings.
	Prophets	**Prophets** are teachers, inspired by God to communicate God's will. These books share messages including instructions, warnings and reminders about how to fulfil God's wishes.
New Testament	**Gospels**	There are four Gospels: Matthew, Mark, Luke, and John. Gospel means 'Good News'. These books record the life, ministry, death and resurrection of Jesus.
	Acts of the Apostles	This book gives details of the growth of the early Church and the things the apostles did during this time.
	Letters	Letters are also called Epistles. These were mostly written by apostles and witnesses of Christ, in particular St Paul. They give guidance on issues faced by the early Church.
	Book of Revelation	This is a very different book to the rest of the New Testament. It is an apocalyptic book, meaning that it describes the end of the world.

Understand

1. What does it mean to say that the Bible is a library of books?
2. Describe three different literary forms in the Bible.
3. Approximately how many human authors of the Bible were there?
4. Why does the Bible, which is written by human authors, have authority?
5. What is the canon of scripture?
6. What are the names of the first five books in the New Testament? You can use the artwork on page 40 to help you answer this question.

You can use the artwork on page 40 to help you answer this question.

Useful vocabulary

prophet: a person inspired by God through the Holy Spirit to share messages from God

Discern

7. 'The Bible is a human creation.' What might a Catholic say to this statement? Give reasons for your ideas and try to use a quotation from *Dei Verbum* 9.
8. Do you think it is important to know that there are different literary forms in the Bible? Give two reasons for your view.

Respond

9. Use a literary form used in the Bible, such as a letter or poem, to explain what scripture means to you.

WHAT CONNECTS THE HEBREW BIBLE AND THE OLD TESTAMENT?

OBJECTIVE

*In this lesson you will learn **why Judaism and Catholicism share some sacred writings.***

Judaism and Christianity have a lot in common. Both religions believe there is only one God, the God of Abraham, Isaac and Jacob. Many of the books of the Old Testament are shared by both Jews (followers of Judaism) and Christians; however they have different names. Jews refer to these books as the **Tanakh**. To Christians they are part of the Old Testament. The Christian Bible also includes a set of books called the New Testament, however Jews do not believe there has been a New Testament. The Old Testament includes more books than the Tanakh and Catholics arrange and interpret the Old Testament in a different way to how Jews arrange and interpret the Tanakh.

Many books of the Old Testament come from the Hebrew scriptures

As Christianity began as a movement within Judaism, it shares some similar beliefs, teachings and practices. One key similarity is that the books from the Tanakh (the Jewish Bible) are included in the Old Testament. These books hold authority within both Judaism and Christianity.

'Tanakh' contains the letters: T, N and K. Each refers to a key part of the Hebrew Bible:

- '**T**orah' which means 'Law' – this section contains the five books of Moses.
- '**N**evi'im' which means 'Prophets' – this section contains the eight books of the Prophets.
- '**K**etuvim' which means 'Writings' – this contains eleven books of stories, Psalms and Proverbs.

Useful vocabulary

Judaism: the religion of the Jewish people, who believe in one God, who revealed the Torah to Moses on Mount Sinai

Tanakh: the Jewish Bible

deuterocanonical texts: a set of books in the Old Testament which are not part of the Jewish Tanakh or Protestant Old Testament

Torah: the first five books of the Jewish holy text, the Tanakh, which Jews believe were given to Moses by God

How do the Tanakh and Old Testament differ?

In total the Tanakh contains 24 books and the Catholic Old Testament has 46. There are differences because the Old Testament has been arranged and ordered differently to the Tanakh. For example, where the Tanakh has one book on the twelve minor prophets, the Old Testament separates this into twelve books. The Old Testament also includes a set of books called the **deuterocanonical texts** which are not part of the Tanakh (or the Protestant Old Testament either). Apart from the first five books (the **Torah**), the order of the Old Testament is different to that of the Tanakh.

The first section of the Tanakh is the Torah. While all sections of the Tanakh are important to Jewish people, this section is seen as very special, because Jews believe that these books were given directly by God to Moses and contain God's law. The next section is Nevi'im, which shows how the Jewish people lived with the laws that God gave them. Some of the books are named after the prophets who wrote them, others such as Judges and Kings tell the stories of hundreds of years of history. The final section, Ketuvim, is a collection of stories, wise sayings (Proverbs) and poetic songs (Psalms). For Catholics, all of the books of the Bible are equally important, but the Gospels are seen as the heart of the Bible because they are the main source Christians have about the life, ministry, death and resurrection of Jesus.

How do Jews and Catholics interpret these books differently?

For Catholics, the Old Testament has value in itself, but also because of the way it points towards the New Testament. Catholics interpret the Old Testament as containing many clues to truths that will be revealed, they believe, in the New Testament. For example, Catholics believe that the Old Testament reveals that God has planned for the coming of a **Messiah**, and the New Testament reveals that this Messiah is Jesus.

The Nevi'im describes that there will be a Messiah who will rule justly and bring equality. Jews, however, do not believe that this Messiah is Jesus and they do not accept that a New Testament has been given. Many Jews do not place a focus on interpreting the Tanakh as part of a bigger story about how God plans to save humankind. Rather they see it as describing the special relationship that God has with his chosen people.

Link

Read more about how the Old and New Testament are closely connected on pages 48–49.

Useful vocabulary

Messiah: a Hebrew term meaning 'anointed one'; many Jews interpret the 'Messiah' to be a future leader of the Jewish people who will rule with kindness and justice; for Christians the Messiah is Jesus; the word 'Christ' is the Greek form of the word Messiah

▲ A girl reads from the Torah scrolls in a synagogue (a Jewish place of worship) for Reform Jews

Understand

1 Name the three parts of the Hebrew Bible.

2 How are the Tanakh and the Old Testament similar?

3 Give two differences between the Tanakh and the Old Testament.

4 Identify two reasons why the Tanakh is important for Jews.

Discern

5 'Jesus has made the Old Testament irrelevant for Christians.' Write down your response to this statement giving reasons to explain your ideas.

Respond

6 Do you think it is important to recognise the similarities between Jews and Christians? Explain your ideas.

WHY IS THE OLD TESTAMENT IMPORTANT FOR CATHOLICS?

Even though the Old Testament was written before the time of Jesus, it is very important for Catholics. It describes the beginning of God's relationship with humans, and it contains covenants and prophecies that Catholics believe Jesus fulfils in the New Testament. It also contains valuable prayers and wisdom that remain a special part of Catholic worship. The New Testament teaches Catholics about the life, ministry, death and resurrection of Jesus, but the Old Testament helps them to understand the whole story of **salvation** history.

How does the Bible reveal God's plan?

The Old Testament is the first part of the Bible as it shows the beginning of God's **revelation** to humans which unfolds God's plan for humanity. The first book in the Bible is Genesis. Genesis 1 and 2 outline God's creation of a perfect world. In Genesis 3, the story of The Fall shows an end to this perfection as humans disobey God. This leads to a great distance between God and humans and the need for them to be saved from their own, now sinful nature.

The Old Testament includes covenants and prophecies which show God's continuing love for humans and explain what people need to do to be close to God. The Old Testament reveals to Christians what God has planned for them: the coming of the Messiah. Catholics believe this Messiah was Jesus, who will grant them salvation.

The New Testament is the second part of the Bible, and reveals details of Jesus' life, ministry, death and resurrection and the spread of the early Church. Jesus often refers to the Old Testament in his teachings, showing his followers that it remains relevant to them and to him. In the New Testament, the writers reveal how Jesus fulfils God's promises given in the Old Testament. The Old Testament helps Catholics to understand Jesus and his mission. Catholics believe that both Testaments together show exactly what God wants to reveal for the purpose of salvation.

Useful vocabulary
salvation: the process of being saved from sin and returning to God through his grace
revelation: the way in which God is made known to humans, which Catholics believe is most perfectly done through Jesus

▲ The Transfiguration, *a painting by Raffaello Sanzio. It shows Jesus with two prophets of the Old Testament, Elijah and Moses, during the Transfiguration (when Jesus was shown to be the Messiah)*

The Old Testament has intrinsic value for Catholics

For Catholics, the Old Testament has 'intrinsic value'. This means that it is essential and valuable in its own right. The following quotation from the Catechism explains why it has this value.

> Catholics believe that the central figure of the Old Testament is Jesus, even though he is not named. The New Testament teaches that the Old Testament should be read with Jesus in mind so that Catholics can understand what it is teaching them about Jesus.

> 'Christians therefore read the Old Testament in the light of Christ crucified and risen… the Old Testament retains its own intrinsic value as Revelation reaffirmed by our Lord himself. Besides, the New Testament has to be read in the light of the Old. Early Christian catechesis made constant use of the Old Testament. As an old saying put it, the New Testament lies hidden in the Old and the Old Testament is unveiled in the New.'
>
> *Catechism of the Catholic Church 129*

> Jesus himself stated that the Old Testament is important, as it is a way in which God makes himself known to human beings. It therefore helps Catholics to understand God and his actions.

> The Old and New Testaments are tightly connected. The New Testament shows the promises and teachings of the Old Testament being fulfilled. Jesus and the early Church used the Old Testament as the foundation of their teachings, which they then developed further.

> The Old Testament holds the clues as to what will happen in the New Testament. In the New Testament these clues are fully revealed and promises and prophecies are fulfilled. The Old and New Testaments are two halves of the whole story of salvation.

Catholics believe that the Old Testament is important because God and God's plans for humankind are revealed there. The Youth Catechism teaches that 'without the Old Testament, we cannot understand Jesus' (YC 17).

Understand

1 Explain one way in which the Old and New Testaments are different.
2 What does 'salvation' mean?
3 What do we mean when we say something has intrinsic value?
4 What does CCC 129 show about the importance of the Old Testament?

Discern

5 'The Old Testament is not important for Catholics.' Write a paragraph explaining how a Catholic might respond to this statement, using evidence to support the arguments you make.

Respond

6 Do you think that the Old Testament is an important part of the Bible? What would the Bible be like without it? Explain your ideas.

WHAT DOES IT MEAN THAT SCRIPTURE IS INSPIRED?

For Catholics, the Bible is the word of God. They believe that although humans wrote the Bible, they were guided by God. The authors' words are what God wanted, or inspired, them to write. Catholics believe that scripture needs to be read in the context in which it was written, but that it is without error in the truths it reveals. The Bible shares God's messages in the words of humans to help guide humans to behave in the ways that God wants, so they can be saved from sin and achieve salvation.

All scripture is 'God-breathed'

As we know, Catholics believe that the scriptures were written by humans in particular places and times in history, using their own unique gifts and talents to do so. However, Catholics believe that God is the true author behind these scriptures and that the people he chose wrote what God wanted them to – God inspired the writers of scripture to know what to write.

Catholics believe that when God created Adam by breathing life into him, God's breath or spirit was shared with all humans. God's spirit, the Holy Spirit, is sent as a guide to humans and this is seen most clearly in the Bible writers: their words are God's breath.

> " 'All Scripture is breathed out by God and profitable for teaching, for reproof, for correction, and for training in righteousness, that the man of God may be complete, equipped for every good work.'
>
> *2 Timothy 3:16–17*

This means that every book of the Bible is inspired by God. Each book has a special authority and can be used for teaching, helping people to develop **morals** and showing them how to live a good life.

God's inspiration is shown in different ways in the scriptures:

- **Prophets** were the inspired spokespersons of God, whose job it was to pass on warnings and messages to people.
- The Gospels contain the record of the life, ministry, death and resurrection of Jesus, who Catholics believe is the Word made flesh, God incarnate. Catholics believe that Jesus is present with his Church through the sacraments and in the scriptures, and that through these God continues to speak to Catholics, guiding how they live and act.
- The **apostles** wrote letters to the early Church and were inspired by the Holy Spirit so that they could teach the word of God.

Scripture is without error

In 1967, Catholic leaders met at a special meeting known as the Second Vatican Council. They talked about the relationship between the Catholic Church and the modern world. Sixteen important documents were written, including *Dei Verbum* which focused on the word of God and how God's word is revealed to Catholics. *Dei Verbum 11* states:

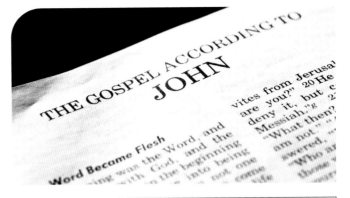

> 'they, as the true authors, **consigned to writing everything** and **only those things** which **He wanted**.'

This means that because the Bible writers were inspired by the Holy Spirit, they wrote only what God wanted them to write.

> 'it follows that the **books of Scripture** must be acknowledged as **teaching solidly, faithfully and without error that truth** which **God wanted** to put into sacred writings for the **sake of salvation**.'

This means that, due to the inspiration of the Holy Spirit, the biblical writers also wrote, without error or mistake, exactly what God wanted to reveal to help humans to achieve salvation.

Scripture guides Catholics towards salvation

Catholics believe that God has a loving plan of salvation for all humans that is communicated through the Bible. Salvation is the belief that through the sacrifice of Jesus on the cross, humans were saved from sin and its consequences. This is called **redemption** and means that by his death and resurrection, Jesus restored humanity's damaged relationship with God following The Fall, and offered them the potential of an eternity with God. Those who accept God's gift of salvation in Jesus can enter heaven.

Catholics believe it makes sense that the authors of the Bible were inspired to write only what God wanted them to, so that humans could understand exactly how to achieve salvation. If the Bible contained errors, it would undermine its authority as the word of God. Catholics believe that God is perfect and all-loving, so the Bible reflects this in its teachings and contains deep truths to help humans on their path.

Useful vocabulary

morals: standards of behaviour; knowing right from wrong

apostles: important early Christian teachers or missionaries, who Jesus sent to spread the Good News; the twelve chief disciples of Jesus

redemption: the belief that Jesus paid the 'ransom' to free humans from sin by dying on the cross

Understand

1 What does the word 'inspired' mean for Catholics?

2 Why do Catholics believe that the Bible has a special authority?

3 Explain what it means to say that scripture is inspired and without error. Use the quotes from the Bible and from *Dei Verbum* in your answer.

Discern

4 'The author of the Bible is God.' Give one reason to agree with this statement and one reason to disagree.

Respond

5 What might you ask about the Bible, if it is said to be an inspired text?

WHAT IS SACRED SCRIPTURE AND SACRED TRADITION?

OBJECTIVE

In this lesson you will explore **the relationship between scripture and tradition in the Catholic Church.**

We have learned that scripture is important because Catholics believe it is the word of God, but alongside this, **tradition** is considered equally important as it is also believed to be the word of God. Tradition refers to the belief that Jesus is continually present with the Church, in its sacraments and teachings, passed on through the apostles to each new generation. This means that because of the continued presence of Jesus as the living Word of God, that sacred tradition has the same authority as the Bible.

What is sacred tradition?

Sacred tradition, also known as Apostolic Tradition, comes down from the original preaching and actions of the apostles. The Bible teaches that Jesus chose 12 apostles and gave them the authority to instruct his followers with his teachings. After Jesus ascended to heaven, the apostles were filled with the Holy Spirit during **Pentecost** (Acts 2:1–4). Catholics believe this gave them even more authority, and that the teachings they passed down are holy. Some were written down, but many were shared by word of mouth through the generations. These include teachings on the **sanctity** of life, the Creeds, the sacraments and the Mass.

▲ *This image shows Mary and the apostles being filled with the Holy Spirit during Pentecost*

What is the relationship between scripture and tradition?

Catholics believe both scripture and tradition are authoritative as they both come from God. *Dei Verbum*, the document 'Word of God' which we met earlier, shows this very clearly:

The source of both scripture and tradition is God.

" 'For both of them, flowing from the same divine wellspring, in a certain way merge into unity and tend toward the same end… it is not from Sacred Scripture alone that the Church draws her certainty … both sacred tradition and Sacred Scripture are to be accepted and venerated with the same sense of loyalty and reverence.'

Dei Verbum 9

Together they give the whole truth of God and salvation.

Both lead a person to God and salvation.

Catholics believe both are equally important to the Church.

Useful vocabulary

tradition: also known as Apostolic Tradition, these are actions and teachings of Jesus faithfully passed on through the sacraments and teachings of the Church

Pentecost: Christian festival seen as the birthday of the Church, when the Holy Spirit came down to the apostles; also a Jewish festival known as Shavuot, celebrating the harvest

sanctity: the state of being holy

Revelation through events and experiences

When God reveals to human beings things they could never know without God's intervention, this is known as 'special revelation'. For Catholics, special revelation is found in both scripture and tradition. Catholics believe that the whole of the Bible is God's word speaking to humans, revealing the divine nature and plan.

Tradition is also seen as the word of God allowing the revelation of God through the Church's faithful passing on of the celebration of the sacraments, and the teachings of the apostles from one generation to the next. Catholics believe that, together, scripture and tradition help them to understand God and live faithfully, so that they can achieve salvation.

Understand

1 What is meant by 'sacred tradition'?
2 Summarise what *Dei Verbum* 9 teaches about sacred scripture and tradition.
3 What does 'special revelation' mean?
4 Where is special revelation found?

Discern

5 Do you think it is necessary to have tradition? Explain your view.

Respond

6 How do you think traditions can be passed on from one generation to the next?

HOW ARE SCRIPTURE, TRADITION AND THE MAGISTERIUM CONNECTED?

The Catholic Church teaches that God's revelation is communicated in two ways: through scripture and tradition – and each of these is interpreted by the **magisterium**. Catholics believe all three – scripture, tradition and magisterium – must be used together to allow the Catholic Church to fully understand, interpret and expand their beliefs. They are like a three-legged stool which needs all three legs for it to stand – if one leg is removed, the stool loses its strength and falls down. It is the same for the Church: the three foundations of scripture, tradition and magisterium give the Church strength and authority.

What is the magisterium?

The term 'magisterium' comes from the Latin '*magister*' meaning teacher or master, but the magisterium isn't a person or a group of people; it is the actual *authority* of the Church to teach, by which we mean the thing that gives the Church the power to speak on behalf of God. Catholics believe this authority comes from God through Jesus. The Bible teaches that Jesus chose St Peter from his twelve apostles to lead and be the foundation of the Church, essentially to be the first **Pope**. Peter and the apostles were given authority by Jesus to instruct his followers, and this authority was made stronger when the apostles were given the Holy Spirit during Pentecost.

Catholics believe that every Pope since Peter has inherited this authority, and every **bishop** since the apostles has continued the work of the twelve to faithfully guide and teach the Church. This is explained in the Catechism:

> " 'the task of giving an **authentic interpretation of the Word of God**, whether in its **written form or in the form of Tradition**, has been entrusted to the **living teaching office of the Church alone**.'
>
> *Catechism of the Catholic Church 85*

For Catholics, this means that the Pope and bishops have the authority to explain the word of God and teach about faith and moral issues and, most importantly, that these teachings can be relied upon by Catholics.

Useful vocabulary

magisterium: from the Latin term *magister*, meaning teacher or master; it is the authority of the Church to teach

Pope: the head of the Catholic Church, who continues as the successor of St Peter and is responsible for the emotional and spiritual needs of the Church

bishop: the head of a local area in the Catholic Church (called a diocese), who continues the work of the apostles

The relationship between scripture, tradition and the magisterium

Scripture, tradition and the magisterium have a special relationship within the Catholic Church. Scripture and tradition give a full account of Jesus, the history and the teachings of the Church and both are considered the word of God by Catholics. The magisterium, guided by the Holy Spirit, gives the bishops the authority to faithfully and accurately interpret both scripture and tradition, so Catholics can have a stronger relationship with God and the Church.

> " 'so that **led by the light of the Spirit of truth**, they may in proclaiming it **preserve this word of God faithfully, explain it, and make it more widely known**.'
>
> *Dei Verbum 9*

The magisterium is guided by the Holy Spirit, which means it can only teach what is right and true. It teaches Catholics the word of God. It also helps Catholics to accurately follow God's word, as it explains it and helps to share it with others.

▲ *A close-up from a fifteenth-century painting which shows Church leaders*

Understand

1 What is the magisterium?

2 Who is considered the first Pope?

3 Describe the relationship between scripture, tradition and magisterium. In your answer refer to *Dei Verbum* 9 (quoted on pages 53 and 55).

Discern

4 'The Bible alone is the word of God.' Give one reason to agree with this statement and one reason to disagree.

Respond

5 Do you think it is helpful to have more than one form of guidance to help you in life? Why do you think this?

HOW DO CATHOLICS USE SCRIPTURE IN THE MASS?

OBJECTIVES

In this lesson you will learn about **the structure of the Catholic Mass and the importance of the Liturgy of the Word.**

Catholics believe that Mass is the greatest form of worship and a vital way to connect with God and the wider community through the sacrifice of Jesus. Mass is a form of liturgical worship, which means a structured form of public worship. The Bible is central to the Mass and is used most clearly in the **Liturgy of the Word**, one of the two main parts of the Mass along with the **Liturgy of the Eucharist**.

The structure of the Mass

The Mass is a Catholic celebration that is carried out all over the world, which creates a deep and important connection with God and within the Catholic community. CCC 1346 states that in Mass 'the table of the Word of the Lord and the Body of the Lord' are found. This refers to the two great parts of the Mass, the Liturgy of the Word and the Liturgy of the Eucharist, each of which bring Catholics closer to God.

In the Liturgy of the Word Catholics hear the words of Jesus (the Word of God) and speak to him in the responses they give. In the Liturgy of the Eucharist Catholics physically unite with Jesus (as the Body of Christ). For Catholics, Mass requires both liturgies, as together they offer spiritual nourishment. The boxes below show how the Mass can be divided into four main parts:

> **Link** 🔗
>
> Read more about the Liturgy of the Eucharist on page 111 and liturgical worship on pages 112–113.

Introductory Rites

- The community gather and make the sign of the cross. This shows that they are gathered together in prayer throughout the Mass.
- The priest greets the **congregation** in Christ's name. Catholics believe that Jesus speaks through the person of the priest during the Mass.
- The Penitential Rite invites people to recall their sins and ask for forgiveness.
- The Gloria, a Christian hymn, is sung on Sundays and feast days.
- The Collect is said, which is a prayer that collects the prayers of the congregation and offers them to God.

Liturgy of the Word

- At the heart of the Liturgy of the Word is the proclamation of the Gospel. Before the Gospel is read, a psalm will be sung and there will be one or two readings from other parts of the Bible. The readings are usually done by people from the congregation. The Gospel is always proclaimed by a priest or a deacon.
- A homily to help listeners understand the scripture in the Liturgy of the Word is given by the priest or deacon.
- The Nicene Creed, the main statement of Christian belief, is recited by the congregation on Sundays or feast days.
- The Prayer of the Faithful is said, which is offered for the needs of the community and the world.

Liturgy of the Eucharist

- The bread and wine are brought to the altar.
- The priest says the Eucharistic prayer in which he asks God to send the Holy Spirit to change the bread and wine into the body and blood of Christ. This process is known as transubstantiation.
- Jesus is then really present in the **consecrated** (blessed) bread and wine, such that, though they still look and taste like bread and wine, they are really his body and blood.
- The priest and ministers offer the body and blood of Christ to the congregation to consume. This is called the Communion Rite.

Concluding Rites

- The priest gives a final blessing to the congregation.
- After the final blessing, the priest sends them out into the world to do God's work, using the words of dismissal.

The Mass is central to Catholic prayer

The Mass is central to Catholic prayer as Catholics believe there is no greater act of prayer than the Mass itself. From the opening prayer of Mass to its concluding prayer, Mass is seen as one continuous raising of hearts and minds to God. Catholics make the sign of the cross to show that they are praying in God. Prayers said during Mass have different purposes: to give thanks, to praise, to intercede and to unite those in worship.

The importance of scripture in Mass

Mass is entirely connected to sacred scripture. Using the words of the Bible in the Mass helps Catholics to connect and understand what God expects of them. Catholics believe that in the Liturgy of the Word God speaks to them through the words of the Bible and the Holy Spirit opens their hearts and minds to the living Word of God. Catholics are spiritually fed, as hearing the words of both Testaments makes the life, ministry, death and **resurrection** of Christ meaningful and relatable. Jesus teaches Christians to live 'by every word that comes from the mouth of God' (Matthew 4:4) so the Liturgy of the Word helps Catholics to follow this commandment. The liturgy of the Eucharist is also founded on scripture. Jesus instituted the Eucharist at the Last Supper, saying 'Do this in remembrance of me' (Luke 22:19).

Understand

1 Name the four parts of the Mass.

2 Explain one way in which scripture is used during the Mass.

3 Identify two reasons why scripture is important in the Liturgy of the Word.

Discern

4 'Only the Liturgy of the Word is needed in Mass.' Give two reasons to disagree with this statement.

Respond

5 **Either:** Have you listened to the Bible being read in Mass? Describe what the experience was like? **Or:** Do you think using scripture in Mass makes scripture more meaningful for Catholics?

HOW IS SCRIPTURE USED IN THE ROSARY?

As well as attending public services in church, Catholics worship God in other ways. One way that Catholics do this is through the Rosary. The Rosary is a set of prayers that is uniquely important to Catholics as it pays respect to Mary and reveals the relationship that she had with her son, Jesus. The Bible does not mention or tell Catholics to pray the Rosary; its use developed from tradition. Each section of the Rosary is completely focused on scripture.

What is the Rosary?

The Rosary is a set of prayers spoken in honour of Mary, and which are usually said while using special **rosary beads**. These have one set of five beads, followed by five sets of ten beads called decades. Each of the ten beads is divided by a single bead, and there is also a crucifix or cross.

One set of five beads

A crucifix (cross)

A set of ten beads, called a decade, divided by a single bead; there are five decades

When praying the Rosary, a person will choose one of the **Mysteries of the Rosary** as a focus for meditation as they pray. These are a series of particular events in the life of Jesus or Mary. Traditional prayers are repeated for each decade (usually one Our Father, ten Hail Marys and one Glory Be).

How is scripture used in the Rosary?

Each Mystery of the Rosary is based on key moments in Jesus or Mary's lives, for example Jesus' Incarnation and suffering and Mary's coronation. When a Catholic prays the Rosary they meditate on a piece of scripture which is connected to their chosen Mystery. This allows Catholics to connect with scripture, and as the prayers are already set, they do not have to worry about making their own prayers but can focus entirely on the scripture in the Mystery.

Each mystery teaches Catholics an important virtue – a positive way to behave. These virtues are revealed by the scripture and are called the **Fruit of the Mystery**. Catholics believe that rather like a tree blesses the farmer with a delicious fruit, scripture blesses Catholics with a fruit of Jesus' teaching.

Useful vocabulary

rosary beads: a string of beads used as an aid to prayer

Mysteries of the Rosary: particular events in the life of Jesus or Mary, known as the Joyful, Sorrowful, Glorious and Luminous Mysteries

Fruit of the Mystery: a virtue or behaviour that helps Catholics to grow in holiness

disciple: someone committed to following the teaching and example of Jesus

The table shows how there are four Mysteries, each broken into five parts and connected with scripture and different virtues.

The Mystery	Each part of the Mystery which is a passage from scripture	Fruit of the Mystery
The Joyful Mysteries	1 The Annunciation 2 The Visitation 3 The Nativity 4 The Presentation in the Temple 5 The Finding in the Temple	1 Humility 2 Love of Neighbour 3 Poverty 4 Obedience 5 Joy in finding Jesus
The Sorrowful Mysteries	1 The Agony in the Garden 2 The Scourging at the Pillar 3 The Crowning with Thorns 4 The Carrying of the Cross 5 The Crucifixion of Jesus	1 Sorrow for Sin 2 Purity 3 Moral Courage 4 Patience 5 Forgiveness
The Glorious Mysteries	1 The Resurrection 2 The Ascension 3 The Descent of the Holy Spirit 4 The Assumption of Mary 5 The Coronation of Mary	1 Faith 2 Hope 3 Love 4 Grace of a happy death 5 Perseverance
The Luminous Mysteries – a later addition by Pope John Paul II in 2002	1 The Baptism of Jesus 2 The Wedding at Cana 3 The Proclamation of the Kingdom of God 4 The Transfiguration 5 The Institution of the Eucharist	1 Openness to the Spirit 2 To Jesus through Mary 3 Trust in God 4 Desire for holiness 5 Adoration

The importance of scripture in the Rosary

Thinking about scripture during the Rosary deepens a person's understanding of that part of the Bible, as well as reminding Catholics of key events in Jesus and Mary's lives. Meditating on the life of Christ helps Catholics relate it to their own life and understand that Christ lived as they did, helping them to form a deep and personal relationship with him. In the Rosary, Catholics are also called to be like Mary: a perfect **disciple**, and to develop the Fruits of the Mysteries. The Rosary also allows Catholics to enter a conversation with God by thinking deeply about the scripture within each mystery; this helps them to uncover truths about the love that God has for humans.

Understand

1 Name the four Mysteries of the Rosary.

2 How is scripture the basis for the Rosary?

3 Identify two reasons why scripture is important in the Rosary.

Discern

4 'The Rosary does not help Catholics connect with scripture.' Give one reason to agree with this statement and one reason to disagree.

5 Do you think the Rosary helps Catholics to be better disciples? Give reasons for your opinion.

Respond

6 Is prayer a part of your life? If so, do words help or hinder you in prayer?

HOW DOES THE BOOK OF KELLS REFLECT THE MEANING OF SCRIPTURE?

The Book of Kells is an ancient and beautiful handwritten book containing the four Gospels. It is vividly and strikingly decorated to bring the words of the Gospels to life. It is believed to have been created around the ninth century and shows how Catholic scripture and beliefs can be expressed in artwork. It is an example of a Christian community's expression of both their faith and their cultural beliefs, ideas and customs.

What is the Book of Kells?

The Book of Kells is an illuminated manuscript, which means the words and pages within it are decorated in an elaborate style to explain and glorify their meaning. It is also sometimes called the Book of Columba because it was created by the medieval monks of St Columba. Many believe the Book of Kells was started on Iona in Scotland at a **monastery** established by Irish monks, before being taken to the monastery at Kells in Ireland where it was completed.

The Book of Kells contains only the four Gospels. Its focus is on the life, ministry, death and resurrection of Jesus. It makes use of amazing calligraphy, so the words themselves are beautifully drawn. However, the main feature of the Book of Kells is the illustrations within it. It is made up of 680 pages, each made of fine parchment. The pages show the Gospels and are elaborately decorated with gold, silver, and vibrant colours. It is one of the greatest pieces of artwork of its time.

Each cross has a Celtic knot pattern in the centre – a design which is common to Celtic cultures, such as from Ireland, Scotland and Wales.

▲ *This page from the Book of Kells shows the Arrest of Christ in the Gospel of St Matthew*

An artistic presentation of sacred scripture

The purpose of the illuminated manuscript is to emphasise the sacred nature of the text by making the stories of the Gospel come to life and appear special and divine. Each page is unique, with images and bold colours designed to draw the viewer into the sacred text.

The Book of Kells was most likely created to be a showpiece in worship, possibly for special celebrations such as Easter. It would most likely not have been read during Mass as there are lots of errors and missing parts within the text. The aim of the Book of Kells was to beautify and glorify the scriptures, to show them honour and respect. The imagery within the Book of Kells also reveals the deeper meaning behind the text, probably to help the viewer understand the religious message behind the words more deeply.

Within the Book of Kells there is some key symbolism from the Gospels:

The Evangelists – the four Gospel writers are depicted throughout the manuscript in various forms, sometimes as humans and sometimes in symbolic form. This emphasises their importance as the people who brought the Gospel to the early Christians.	The Cross – this is used throughout the Book of Kells in various styles. It is the most common and easily recognised symbol of Christianity and is used to show that Jesus was crucified to save humans from sin.	The Chi Rho – these are two Greek letters which form the first part of the word Christ. The symbol is used throughout the Book of Kells to symbolise Jesus.	Numbers – these are used in various ways in the Book of Kells. When objects are grouped into threes, it is often interpreted to be a reference to the Holy Trinity.

A Christian community's expression of faith and culture

The Book of Kells is seen as a cultural treasure because it blends Celtic and Christian styles to reveal how a medieval community worshipped and communicated their beliefs. The Irish influence runs throughout, for example many designs feature the Celtic knot, so it shows the cultural background of the Catholic monastic community who created it.

It also shows the faith of the community as it brings the word of God to life in a visual way. The monks who created the Book of Kells tried to breathe life into the text of the Gospels in the imagery they used, reflecting the idea that Jesus is the living Word of God. The Book of Kells can help Catholics understand more about the mystery of Christ and the teachings of the Gospels. It is also evidence of how the Catholic community has shown dedication and love to Jesus throughout the last two thousand years, in a beautiful work of art that would have taken immense time and hard work to complete.

Useful vocabulary

monastery: a building or buildings where a community of religious brothers or sisters live

Link

Read more about the Trinity on pages 80–83.

Understand

1 What is the Book of Kells?
2 Summarise how the Book of Kells is an artistic presentation of sacred scripture.
3 How does the Book of Kells use symbolism to express Catholic beliefs?

Discern

4 'Bibles do not need pictures as the words are enough.' Write a paragraph to explain how a Catholic might respond to this idea.
5 How well does the Book of Kells show both the faith and the culture of the Christian community who created it?

Respond

6 Has learning about the Book of Kells made you think differently about how we should read the Bible?

WHAT ARE BIBLICAL IDIOMS?

Idioms have been present in language for thousands of years. They are expressions or phrases that do not have literal meanings, but give an idea or meaning that is different from the actual words used, for example, 'It's raining cats and dogs!' As a book that is well-known for telling stories with many layers, the Bible has been the source of many idioms. They are widely used today, though people do not always realise their origin, or that they are referencing scripture. Their use reflects the deep impact that the Bible has had on cultural life through the years.

What are idioms?

Idioms are expressions that should not be taken literally. People use them to communicate deeper meanings but in new and creative ways. They are an important part of how people express themselves and often reflect cultural, historical, and religious influences on societies. They also show that humans are much more than literal beings and enjoy using idioms to paint interesting images with words. Idioms can also reflect that a person is comfortable and confident in using a particular language, as they can express complex ideas using simple sentences. This can result in confusion, or an amusing situation, if non-local speakers do not understand the meaning of these expressions, or try to use them but get muddled up, for example 'It's raining snakes and donkeys!'

Useful vocabulary

biblical idiom: a figurative phrase connected to a passage from the Bible which has a non-literal meaning

Biblical idioms

Since the Bible was first translated and widely published in English in the 1500s, it has had an immense impact on the development of the English language. The Bible became accessible to ordinary people and therefore it became much more widely-read. This resulted in phrases from the Bible being used more commonly in speech and literature, which led to the development of **biblical idioms**.

Link

Read more about the translation of the Bible on pages 42–43.

> 'For it is easier for a camel to go through the eye of a needle than for a rich person to enter the kingdom of God.'
>
> *Luke 18:25*

Biblical idioms have their foundation in scripture, but were developed to be used in everyday life to convey a particular meaning – often different to the meaning in the Bible. They come from both the Old and New Testaments and continue to have a lasting presence in cultural life today.

The table below gives some examples of biblical idioms with their scriptural root, meaning and an example to show how they would be used.

Biblical idiom	Scriptural reference	Meaning	Example
A camel through the eye of a needle	Luke 18:25	Something that is very difficult/nearly impossible to do	'It would be easier to get a camel through the eye of a needle than to fool my mum.'
An eye for an eye	Exodus 21:24	The punishment for a crime should be equal to the crime itself	'You broke my phone, so I'm going to break yours: it's an eye for an eye!'
The blind leading the blind	Matthew 15:14	Someone who tries to teach another person something when they don't have the knowledge themselves	'I would love to help you with your French homework, but it would be like the blind leading the blind.'
Extend an olive branch	Genesis 8:11	Something a person does to bring about peace	'He was sorry he shouted and extended an olive branch by making her a cup of tea.'
By the skin of my teeth	Job 19:20	Just about/barely	'I passed my driving test by the skin of my teeth.'

The presence and impact of biblical idioms in cultural life

Biblical idioms are widely used in cultural life in the UK today. They are found in speech, the media and different types of literature. Biblical idioms reflect the historical and religious influence that the Bible has had on society; over the last two thousand years Christianity has been an essential part of millions of lives. The Church held an important position in how many countries were governed. They cared for the sick and ran schools, and religion was the central focus of many people's lives. Most people attended worship at church, which meant the Church shaped both individuals and wider society. Strong images are often easiest to remember and share, so idioms heard in Mass became imprinted on people's minds and were a normal part of everyday language.

When people use biblical idioms today, they may not know their origin or that they are indirectly referencing the Bible, which shows how deeply the Bible has influenced society. Biblical idioms can refer to both religious and non-religious ideas. This means that they have had an impact outside of Christianity as they have become meaningful turns of phrase for all people, whatever their religious or non-religious outlook, and have become part of everyday language.

Understand

1 What is an idiom?

2 How are biblical idioms different to ordinary idioms?

3 Give three reasons why people might use idioms.

4 Give two examples of biblical idioms. Put them into sentences, different to the examples given, to show how they would be used.

Discern

5 'Biblical idioms are still important today.' Give one reason to agree with this statement and one reason to disagree.

6 Explain two different impacts biblical idioms have on cultural life in the UK today.

Respond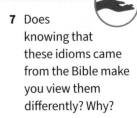

7 Does knowing that these idioms came from the Bible make you view them differently? Why?

ASSESSMENT

Key vocabulary

Write a definition for these key terms.

revelation	*Dei Verbum*	scripture	tradition
magisterium	inspired	canon	Old Testament
New Testament	Hebrew, Aramaic, Greek	Tanakh	Liturgy of the Word

Knowledge check

1 Which of these phrases is the meaning of *Dei Verbum* (the name of a document from the Second Vatican Council)?

  a 'Word of God'

  b 'God-breathed'

  c 'God made flesh'

2 Copy out and complete the following sentence:

The word 'Tanakh' contains letters that refer to the three parts of the Hebrew Bible – Torah, Nevi'im, K..................

3 What was published in 1611 that became the official English Bible of the Protestant Church?

  a The King John Bible

  b The King James Bible

  c The King Edward Bible

4 Approximately how many authors are there of the Bible?

5 What is the Liturgy of the Word?

6 What is the Rosary?

7 What is the purpose of biblical idioms?

8 Describe how the Book of Kells might inspire someone to think or act towards scripture.

9 The magisterium is important to Catholics. Explain the reasons for this.

10 Explain how Catholics use scripture in Mass.

TIP

Try to find a piece of scripture linked to the importance of the magisterium. Use this as the starting point for your answer and give an example of how the magisterium is used.

TIP

Before you start writing make sure that you understand what is meant by 'Mass'. You do not need to write about the order of the Mass, rather you need to focus on where scripture is used within it and why.

Extended writing activity

This assessment is for you to show what you have learned in this chapter and to develop your extended writing skills. Here is a big question:

Explain the role of scripture and tradition for Catholics, and the impact this has on how Catholics practise their faith.

This can be broken down into two smaller questions. Your teacher will direct you to which questions they want you to answer.

TIP

- *Remember that scripture and tradition are different but work together.*
- *Really good answers will explain what scripture and tradition are, what they are for and the importance of each.*

1 **What is the role of scripture and tradition in the Catholic Church?**

You could use 'Point-Evidence-Explain' to write at least one paragraph to answer this question.

Point – make the point for your paragraph

Evidence – give evidence to back up your point

Explain – what the evidence means and how it answers the question

Here is an example:

The role of scripture and tradition is to reveal the word of God to Catholics and to teach them how to live as God wants. Dei Verbum 9 explains that both are the word of God because they flow 'from the same divine wellspring.' For Catholics, this shows that the source of both scripture and tradition is God, and together they can be relied on to give Catholics important truths which God wants to communicate.

1 A **point** is made in this first sentence.

2 There is **evidence** to back up the point in this second sentence.

3 This sentence **explains** what the evidence means and how it answers the question.

Words you could use:

Dei Verbum   inspired   reveal   bishops

Try to write at least one more paragraph about the role of scripture and tradition in the Catholic Church. You might find these sentence starters helpful.

For Catholics scripture is...

Scripture is important because...

Tradition is...

Words you could use:

word of God   apostles   authority
early Church   magisterium

2 **What impact does scripture and tradition have on Catholics today?**

For this question, try to include at least two different suggestions about the impact that scripture and tradition have on Catholics today. You can use the same 'Point-Evidence-Explain' approach here.

Examples you could use:

public worship   the Mass   the Rosary   development of the sacraments
Liturgy of the Word   Liturgy of the Eucharist   prayer

TIP

To remind yourself about how scripture features in the Mass, look back at pages 56–57. To read about how scripture is used in the Rosary, look back at pages 58–59.

GALILEE TO JERUSALEM

Introduction

The Gospels are at the heart of Christianity because they allow people to know Jesus through the life he lived and the words he spoke.

In this chapter we will consider the key question of **who Jesus was**. The scriptures of the Old Testament had prepared the way for a Messiah and Christians believe that this Messiah was Jesus. As well as 'Messiah', Jesus is also known as: 'Son of God', 'Son of Man', 'Christ' and 'Lord'. **But what do these titles actually mean?**

Many Catholics believe that the most important of all of these titles is **Son of God**. That is because understanding Jesus as the Son of God is central to two core Catholic beliefs: **the Holy Trinity** and **the Incarnation**. These teachings affect every aspect of Catholic prayer and life. They are celebrated in Christian festivals such as Christmas. You will explore how these teachings have inspired individual Catholics as well as Christian art, including work by artists such as Andrei Rublev and Meg Wroe.

For a Christian, Jesus' authority comes from the belief that he is God. However, because he is also human, he sets an example that can be followed by every human being. Many Catholics have devoted their lives to following the example of Jesus. This includes Father Mychal Judge, who gave his life in the service of others.

Whenever there is a decision to be made about right and wrong, **Jesus will always be the most important role model for Catholics**. This extends to the world of business today, and while Jesus did not directly address issues of business, he did teach Christians how to choose the right path. Catholics believe that Jesus' perfect example continues to give directions about how to do good in the world today.

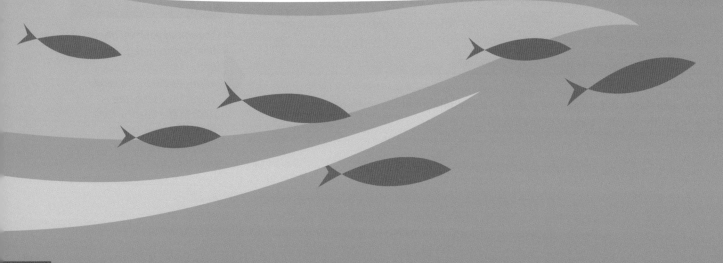

WHAT IS THE INCARNATION?

OBJECTIVES

In this lesson you will learn about the Catholic Church's teaching that God came to earth as a human being: Jesus.

The word 'incarnate' means 'made flesh' and the **Incarnation** refers to the time when God became flesh – in other words, a human being – in Jesus. This is a very important belief for Christians because it shows that while Jesus is truly human, he is at the same time, truly God.

What is the doctrine of the Incarnation?

The Incarnation is an important doctrine (teaching) in Catholicism because it explains how God was physically present on earth in Jesus. Jesus was not a separate being sent to earth by God: he is God. This means that when Christians worship Jesus, they are worshipping God. For Christians therefore, Jesus is worthy of all of the adoration of God because *he is God*. **Christmas** is an important festival for Christians as it celebrates the Incarnation – the coming of God as a human being in the birth of Jesus.

Why did the Incarnation take place?

Christians believe that the Incarnation happened because God loved humans and wanted to repair their broken relationship. Jesus came to earth as a human being to share God's message with humans, revealing God's love for them and offering them the chance of salvation: to be saved from sin. In John's Gospel, Jesus is described as the 'light of the world' (John 8:12) because he shows people the right way to live. It also shows the depth of God's love for human beings in sending Jesus, God's only Son, to save the world through his life, death and resurrection.

What does the Catholic Church teach about the Incarnation?

Revelation means to reveal or share something important. Jesus revealed messages *from* God, but he also *was* God. For this reason, Jesus himself is seen by Christians as the fullness of revelation, in whom God says everything there is to say. The idea of the Incarnation of Jesus being the full revelation of God's message on earth is explained in more detail in the quotation from the Catechism on the opposite page.

> **Useful vocabulary**
>
> **Incarnation:** Christians believe that God became man in the person of Jesus, truly human and truly divine
>
> **Christmas:** a Christian festival that celebrates the Incarnation in the birth of Jesus
>
> **prophet:** a person inspired by God through the Holy Spirit to share messages from God
>
> **divine:** of God

▲ *Many images of the nativity, such as on religious Christmas cards, have a light shining on the baby Jesus to show that he is the 'light of the world'*

> ""In many and various ways God spoke of old to our fathers by the prophets, but in these last days he has spoken to us by a Son." Christ, the Son of God made man, is the Father's one, perfect and unsurpassable Word. In him he has said everything; there will be no other word than this one.'
>
> *Catechism of the Catholic Church 65*

The Catechism refers to a quotation from the Bible which explains how God had sent messengers, or **prophets**, before Jesus. However, Jesus is more than a prophet, he is 'a Son'.

Catholics believe that, before Jesus, God revealed himself gradually and in part to the Jewish people, as recorded in the Old Testament. In the scriptures of the Old Testament, they could read the conversations between God and the prophets, for example. Catholics believe that Jesus is the living Word of God – through him God has given humans everything they need to know to understand God and to achieve salvation. No further words are needed because Jesus reveals every truth and shows exactly what God is like. Because of the Incarnation, human beings become 'partakers of the **divine** nature' (CCC 460), meaning they can have a relationship with God and become more like God.

Here, the Catechism says that the person of Jesus surpasses (or is seen as greater than) the scriptures. Catholics believe he is now 'the Word' because he is the perfect way in which people can know who God is, because Jesus *is* God.

The Nicene Creed and the Incarnation

The Nicene Creed, the main Christian statement of belief, emphasises the importance of the doctrine of the Incarnation for Catholics.

> 'I believe in one Lord Jesus Christ,
> the Only Begotten Son of God,
> born of the Father before all ages.
> God from God, Light from Light,
> true God from true God,
> begotten, not made;
>   consubstantial with the Father;
> through him all things were made.
> For us men and for our salvation
> he came down from heaven,
> and by the Holy Spirit was incarnate
>   of the Virgin Mary,
> and became man.'
>
> *Articles 2–4 of the Nicene Creed*

The Nicene Creed takes each person of the Trinity in turn. The section that explains who Jesus is is the longest because it explains the doctrine of the Incarnation.

This emphasises Jesus being one and the same as God.

This means that Jesus is the Son of the Father (begotten means born) and wasn't created like everything else that exists.

The word 'consubstantial' means that the Son is 'of the same substance' as the Father: they are both God.

God came to earth as Jesus for the sake of humanity and in order to save humanity.

Understand

1 What do the following words mean: Incarnation; consubstantial?

2 Explain the Catholic belief in the Incarnation. In your answer, explain why the Incarnation took place and make reference to the Nicene Creed.

Discern

3 'The doctrine of the Incarnation is easy to understand.' Write a response to this statement and give two reasons to support your argument.

Respond

4 What do you think it means to be truly human and truly divine?

WHO IS JESUS, THE SON OF GOD?

OBJECTIVES

*In this lesson you will learn **why Catholics call Jesus the 'Only Begotten Son of God'**.*

Jesus is called by many titles in the New Testament. One of the most important of these for understanding the Trinity is '**Son of God**'. 'Son of God' does not mean that Jesus is less than God, but rather that he is the Son of the Father: one of the persons of the Trinity, and truly God.

Why do Catholics call Jesus the 'Son of God'?

The Catechism of the Catholic Church includes a number of paragraphs that speak about Jesus as the Son of God. Similarly, the Nicene Creed refers to Jesus as the 'Only Begotten Son of God'. For Catholics, this title puts Jesus on a totally different level to any other human being, even his own mother Mary. Youth Catechism 74 says 'the expression means that of all human beings only Jesus is more than a man'. Other men are 'sons' too, but to be the 'Son of God' is special and unique. This name shows that Jesus is human, but more than this he is one and the same as God, and a person of the **Trinity**.

Link

Read more about Jesus as a person of the Trinity on pages 80–81.

How the title 'Son of God' is used in the Bible

Some parts of the Old Testament talk about what the Messiah will be like or what will happen when the Messiah comes. In Psalms 2:7, there is a prophecy made that God will call the Messiah a 'Son': 'The Lord said to me, "You are my Son; today I have begotten you"'. There is another prediction like this in 2 Samuel 7:14: 'I will be to him a father, and he shall be to me a son'. The passage also talks about discipline and the unconditional love that a parent has for their child.

The baptism of Jesus is an important story in the New Testament. One reason for this is the way in which Jesus is presented, first by his cousin John the Baptist, and then by God the Father. Mark's Gospel opens with a quotation from the Old Testament prophet Isaiah, who speaks of an individual who will 'prepare the way of the Lord' (Mark 1:3). Catholics believe that this is John the Baptist. Mark tells the reader more about John the Baptist, describing his popularity at the time.

▶ *In this stained glass image, John the Baptist pours water over Jesus to baptise him; the Holy Spirit appears as a dove*

But John speaks about his cousin Jesus, saying he is not worthy enough to even tie Jesus' sandals. By this, John means that he is not good enough to be a servant to Jesus – this is how important Jesus is.

Jesus still comes to John for baptism, however. His baptism is described in the Gospel of Mark.

> **'The Baptism of Jesus**
>
> In those days Jesus came from Nazareth of Galilee and was baptised by John in the Jordan. And when he came up out of the water, immediately he saw the heavens being torn open and the Spirit descending on him like a dove. And a voice came from heaven, "You are my beloved Son, with you I am well pleased".'
>
> *Mark 1:9–11*

All three persons of the Trinity are referred to in the account of Jesus' baptism.

God the Father speaks about Jesus as his 'beloved Son', showing that Jesus' relationship with God the Father is unlike any other. While Catholics believe that all human beings can refer to God as 'Father', Jesus shares a closeness with God the Father like no one else.

What does it mean to be the Son of God?

Jesus' title 'Son of God' does not refer to physical parenting, but a relationship in another sense. It is the claim that Jesus is of the same nature as God and therefore part of God in the Trinity. Jesus is therefore divine and Catholics would think Jesus worthy of the adoration that God deserves.

Understand

1 Why do Catholics call Jesus the 'Only Begotten Son of God'?

2 What does the title 'Son of God' tell us about Jesus?

3 What was predicted in the Old Testament about God's relationship to the Messiah?

4 Who is present at Jesus' baptism?

5 Identify three things that happen at Jesus' baptism.

6 What does the voice from heaven say, and why is this important?

Discern

7 'Understanding the Incarnation helps you to understand the title "Son of God" better.' How far do you agree with this statement?

Respond

8 Read the full account of Jesus' baptism in Mark 1:1–11. Write an account of Jesus' baptism as if you were an eyewitness. How do the people in the crowd react? What about John and Jesus?

WHAT DID ARIUS TEACH ABOUT JESUS?

OBJECTIVES

In this lesson you will explore **how the Catholic Church settled differences of opinion about who Jesus was.**

After Pentecost the apostles spread out and converted people to Christianity in distant lands. All these new Christians belonged to the same Church, but some of them began to have new ideas about who Jesus was. Some of these ideas were very different to the original teachings of the Church and so meetings of church leaders began to take place in order to discuss these challenges. The First Council of Nicaea discussed the ideas of a man called Arius.

Arius and Christianity in the fourth century

After Jesus' life, death and resurrection came the event of Pentecost. This event gave the apostles the courage to start to convert people to Christianity. They began their **mission** to travel to different places, especially around Southern Europe and North Africa, telling people about Jesus. Soon more and more people from different countries were becoming Christian. Over the course of time, however, some of the more complicated teachings caused debate. This included the teachings about who Jesus actually was.

Arius was a Christian elder who lived in the fourth century in Alexandria in Egypt. At this time, everyone who was Christian belonged to the same Church, however, with so much physical distance between places it was difficult to keep every teaching exactly the same – and many new Christians had new ideas to share. During these years the doctrines of the Church that had always been believed were just beginning to be written down so that there would be a record of Church teachings. The ideas of Arius were a test of certain key Church teachings, as Arius suggested something quite different.

What did Arius say that caused disagreement?

Arius made several suggestions:

Arius said that Jesus did not just exist as God did – he was created *by* God.	→	This would mean that Jesus was relying on God the Father to exist. That would make God the Father more powerful than Jesus and therefore more important.	→	Arius argued that Jesus' life started and came to an end like any human being, so that made God the Father alone the Almighty one.	→	If this was the case, Jesus could not have the same nature as God the Father, which meant he was not divine and the Incarnation could not be true.

Useful vocabulary

mission: a great task or purpose which, in Christianity, is given by God

Arianism: the belief put forward by Arius in the fourth century that Jesus was not divine

heresy: an opinion or belief that goes against Church teaching, or the denial of a revealed truth

Link

Read more about Pentecost on pages 52–53.

St Athanasius, who also lived in Alexandria, disagreed with **Arianism** strongly.

Arianism did not suggest that Christians stop worshipping Jesus; Arius thought that Christians should still worship the Son and the Father.	St Athanasius argued that this was the same as worshipping more than one God, because if God the Father was one God, then God the Son must be a different God.	This would be a sin and **heresy**. It also hugely decreased the importance of Jesus and the sacrifice he made if Jesus was no longer as important as God the Father.

What was the Catholic Church's reaction?

The Catholic Church decided that Arius was guilty of heresy. A heretic is someone who is baptised a Catholic but then does not accept a necessary part of the faith; in this case Arius did not accept that Jesus was God. As other people started to consider and accept Arius' views, the Church held a meeting in order to discuss the matter further. This took place in Nicaea (which is in modern day Turkey) in AD 325.

The First Council of Nicaea did not agree with Arius and forced him to leave Alexandria to show it was a serious step for a Catholic to question the doctrines of the Church. The Creed of Nicaea was also written, which later became the Nicene Creed. The Church wanted an official statement of faith to make the doctrines clearer and to recognise that Jesus was divine: true God, as well as truly man. We can see in the Nicene Creed how the beliefs of Arianism are directly addressed and rejected, confirming the Church's doctrine that Jesus is God.

> I believe in one Lord Jesus Christ, the Only Begotten Son of God, born of the Father before all ages.
>
> **God from God, Light from Light, true God from true God, begotten, not made**, consubstantial with the Father; through him all things were made.
>
> *Articles 2 and 3 of the Nicene Creed*

▲ *A fresco showing the First Council of Nicaea in AD 325, from the Basilica of St Nicholas, an Eastern Orthodox church in Turkey*

Understand

1 What was Arianism?

2 Why did the Church reject Arius' ideas about Jesus?

3 Why was the Nicene Creed written?

4 What does it mean to say that Jesus is true God and true man?

Discern

5 Do you agree with St Athanasius that Arianism meant worshipping more than one God? Explain your ideas.

6 Do you think the Church responded correctly to Arianism? Give reasons for your answers.

Respond

7 Do you think that in a religion, it's important that everyone holds the same beliefs?

OBJECTIVES

In this lesson you will learn what Jesus' title 'Son of Man' means.

WHO IS JESUS, THE SON OF MAN?

In the Bible, Jesus never explicitly uses grand titles to describe himself. Sometimes he agrees with what others say he is, but when he describes himself, '**Son of Man**' is the most common title he uses. When he uses this title he is sometimes using it to refer to himself as a humble human being, and sometimes he uses it to describe his unique role in human history.

How the title 'Son of Man' is used in the Old Testament

The title 'Son of Man' is used in both the Old Testament and New Testament. In the Old Testament, for example in Psalm 8:4, it literally means 'human being'. However, an extra meaning is given to the title through a vision had by David, described in the book of Daniel. He describes the Messiah coming to earth: 'behold, with the clouds of heaven there came one like a son of man… And to him was given a dominion and glory' (Daniel 7:13–14). Catholics believe this confirms that Jesus is the Messiah – he came to earth as a human being, but from God in heaven and was therefore more than a man. Both Psalm 8 and Daniel 7 talk about the majesty and glory of God, however the title 'Son of Man' contrasts with this idea and is an important reminder for Catholics of the humanity of Jesus, despite his role as the Messiah.

How Jesus uses the title 'Son of Man' in the New Testament

In Mark's Gospel Jesus often uses the title 'Son of Man' to talk about himself. As the vision described in Daniel suggests, the title reveals the nature of Jesus as both a man and as the Messiah. However, the reason why Jesus uses this title instead of others, such as Messiah, is open to debate. Perhaps it is because he wants to emphasise his humility, or avoid using a title that others might misunderstand.

Suffering and service

In the story of the Request of James and John (Mark 10:35–45), Jesus uses the title 'Son of Man' to show the example he wants to set. James and John ask if they can sit either side of Jesus when he sits in glory in heaven. Jesus points out that this is not what his ministry is all about; in fact it is the opposite. He has come to show how to endure suffering in the **service** of others.

> " ‖ 'For even the Son of Man came not to be served but to serve, and to give his life as a ransom for many.'
> *Mark 10:45*

'Ransom' refers to the sacrifice Jesus will make on the cross to fix the damaged relationship between God and humanity.

Useful vocabulary

Son of Man: a title for Jesus which suggests that he is both divine and human; it connects to the idea of him as a Messiah

service: supporting the needs of others and putting them before our own; this might include physical and spiritual needs, for example

eschatology: the 'discussion of the last things', this includes death, Judgement, the soul and the end of time

Last Day of Judgement: the Jewish and Christian belief that there will be a day at the end of time when all people will be raised up and judged for their actions

Link

Read more about the Messiah on pages 70 and 76–77 and in Chapter 2 on pages 47–48.

This looks ahead to Jesus' suffering and final act of service in giving his life for humanity. In this passage, Jesus is trying to explain to James and John that serving other people and putting them first is more important than any other act.

Authority

The story of Jesus healing a man who was paralysed in Mark 2:1–12 shows Jesus' authority to do things that people at the time would only expect God to be able to do. He acts with the authority of God when he says, 'But that you may know that the Son of Man has authority on earth to forgive sins' (Mark 2:10). For Jewish people at that time, this would have been an astonishing and disrespectful thing to say, as they believed only God could forgive sins. Jesus uses the title 'Son of Man' here as a claim to his divine authority. He acts with the authority of God, but he acts in service to others as a man.

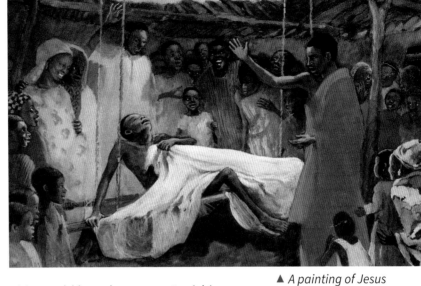

▲ *A painting of Jesus healing a man who was paralysed, from the* Life of Jesus Mafa *project*

Eschatology

An important part of Christianity is **eschatology**: the teachings about what will happen at the end of time. Some of these teachings come from the things Jesus said. For example, Jesus referred to himself as the 'Son of Man' when he described what will happen on the **Last Day of Judgement**, a day at the end of time when Christians believe all people will be raised up and judged for their actions.

> " '"… you will see the Son of Man seated at the right hand of Power, and coming with the clouds of heaven".'
>
> *Mark 14:61–62*

Here, the way 'Son of Man' is used reflects the connection to the Messiah that is made in the Old Testament book of Daniel, emphasising Jesus' power and authority as God.

Understand

1 In the Old Testament, who is the 'son of man' referred to in David's vision?

2 How does Jesus correct James and John's understanding in the story of the Request of James and John?

3 What does the story of Jesus healing a man who was paralysed reveal about Jesus?

Discern

4 'The title Son of Man suggests that Jesus was not God, but just a nice man.' Write a response to this statement that a Catholic might make.

Respond

5 Do you think humility is an important quality for a person to have? If so, why?

WHO IS JESUS, THE CHRIST AND SON OF DAVID?

One of the important titles used for Jesus is **'Christ'**. The word 'Christ' comes from the Greek word *chrīstós* for the Hebrew title 'Messiah', which means 'anointed one'. To be anointed is to be a person chosen by God. In the Old Testament there are prophecies made about a Messiah, who will be descended from David. For Christians, Jesus is that Messiah: the Christ.

What does 'Christ' mean?

There are many times in the New Testament when Jesus is referred to as 'Jesus Christ', for example in the opening of Mark's Gospel, which says: 'The beginning of the gospel of Jesus Christ, the Son of God' (Mark 1:1). 'Christ' is not a middle name or surname, but instead it is an important title from the Hebrew 'Messiah'. The title 'Messiah' itself is not used in the Old Testament, but the Old Testament does often talk about a chosen person who will come in the future who will be sent by God. For Catholics, the title 'Christ' shows that Jesus was not only chosen by God, but that he fulfils what was being prophesised in the Old Testament about the Messiah.

In the Old Testament, priests, prophets and kings were anointed with oil to mark their setting aside for a special purpose. There was an expectation at the time of Jesus that a Messiah would come who would fulfil these three functions perfectly in himself. Christians believe this person was Jesus which is why they call him Christ, meaning 'the anointed one.' He is the perfect priest, prophet and king, and all of this is summed up by using the title 'Jesus Christ'.

> '**Why is Jesus called "Christ"?**
>
> … "Jesus is the Christ" expresses the core of the Christian faith: Jesus, the simple carpenter's son from Nazareth, is the long-awaited Messiah and Saviour.'
>
> *Youth Catechism 73*

Useful vocabulary

Christ: a title for Jesus, which means he was chosen by God

How does the title 'Christ' link to the Old Testament and to David?

There are lots of books of the Old Testament in which predictions are made about the Messiah. For example:

> 'And your house and your kingdom shall be made sure for ever before me. **Your throne shall be established for ever.**'
>
> *2 Samuel 7:16*

> 'Then I will establish **your royal throne over Israel for ever**, as I promised **David your father**, saying, "You will not lack a man on the throne of Israel".'
>
> *1 Kings 9:5*

For Christians, Jesus fulfils these predictions. In 2 Samuel and 1 Kings, there is a prophecy that the Messiah will be descended from David, who was a king of Israel. Matthew's Gospel opens with a long family history of Jesus, showing the link from Abraham (the father of the Jewish nation) and David to Joseph, who marries Mary and helps to raise Jesus. Matthew is mainly writing for a Jewish audience who would have been aware that the Messiah should have links to David, so by writing this history, Matthew is making this connection very clear.

In 2 Samuel and 1 Kings there are references made to a throne and to the reign of the Messiah lasting forever. For Christians, describing Jesus as the Christ is recognising him as a king who will remain king for eternity. This does not mean that Jesus physically sits on a throne and wears a crown. Jesus' reign is more metaphorical. For Christians, he is the king and lord of all, with complete and ultimate authority and that continues after our life on earth has ended.

How does the New Testament show Jesus as the Christ and Son of David?

In Mark 10:46–52, Jesus is met by a blind beggar called Bartimaeus who calls out to Jesus, 'Son of David, have mercy on me!' Bartimaeus is asking Jesus to heal him. This is significant because it is a recognition by Bartimaeus that Jesus is the Messiah. The miracle itself has an important meaning. The blind man is physically able to see once Jesus performs the miracle, however, the miracle also enables him to 'see Jesus' in a spiritual sense – as the anointed one, ancestor of David, and Messiah: the Christ.

The story of Palm Sunday appears next in Mark's Gospel after the healing of Bartimaeus. In this story, crowds of people welcome Jesus into Jerusalem, scattering palm branches in his path as he humbly rides in on a donkey. In Zechariah in the Old Testament, the Messiah's arrival was predicted exactly as Jesus fulfilled: 'Shout aloud, O daughter of Jerusalem! Behold, your king is coming to you; righteous and having salvation is he, humble and mounted on a donkey' (Zechariah 9:9).

Jesus does not travel in grandeur as you might expect from a king, but yet the crowds shout, 'Hosanna! Blessed is he who comes in the name of the Lord! Blessed is the coming kingdom of our father David!' (Mark 11:9–10). There seems to be a recognition of who Jesus is at this point and a link is made to the Messiah, again through the reference to David. However, it will not be long before the same crowd shout for Jesus' execution on Good Friday. This crowd do not seem to really have a true understanding of who Jesus is, unlike Bartimaeus. Bartimaeus' faith means that he can truly see what and who Jesus is, so he leaves everything to follow him.

▲ A painting by Elizabeth Wang showing Jesus being welcomed into Jerusalem on Palm Sunday

Discern

6 Do you think Christians should always refer to Jesus as 'Jesus Christ'? Give a reason to support your answer.

Respond

7 Do you think it is easier or harder to accept Jesus as the Messiah in our modern world compared to when Jesus lived?

Understand

1 How are the words 'Christ' and 'Messiah' linked?

2 Why do Christians use the word 'Christ' after Jesus' name?

3 What was predicted about the Messiah in the Old Testament?

4 What is the connection between Jesus and David?

5 How do the crowds show an awareness of who Jesus is on Palm Sunday?

WHO IS JESUS, THE LORD?

The title '**Lord**' can be used in Britain in a non-religious way to show respect when addressing people with certain titles such as earls, viscounts or barons. However, as a title for Jesus and for God the Father, it shows they have absolute superiority and divinity.

What does 'Lord' mean and when is it used?

In Catholicism, 'Lord' is used to refer to the divine; it is a title of majesty which is used in both the Old Testament and New Testament. This title is used in a way to show that God, or Jesus, has complete authority and power and is superior to all.

How the title 'Lord' is used in the Old Testament

In Exodus, God appears to Moses in the story of the Burning Bush to tell Moses of the plan to rescue the Jewish people from slavery in Egypt.

> " 'God said to Moses, "I AM WHO I AM." And he said, "Say this to the people of Israel: 'I AM has sent me to you'." God also said to Moses, "Say this to the people of Israel: 'The LORD, the God of your fathers, the God of Abraham, the God of Isaac, and the God of Jacob, has sent me to you'."'
>
> *Exodus 3:14–15*

In this story, God reveals his personal name to Moses. The four letters that make up God's personal name in Hebrew are equivalent to the English letters YHWH, whose literal meaning is 'I Am'. This personal name for God is never said out loud by Jewish people, even to this day, out of respect for God's name. Most Christian Bibles also use the word LORD (all in capitals) to represent this Hebrew word when they translate it into English. So, slowly the word LORD became the way of referring personally to God. Hence when it is used by early Christians to describe Jesus, it is a way of expressing their belief that Jesus is God. For example, St Paul writes in his letter to the Phillipians: 'at the name of Jesus every knee should bow... and that every tongue should confess that Jesus Christ is Lord, to the glory of God the Father.' (Philippians 2:10–11) What he means is that everyone should recognise that Jesus is God, alongside the Father.

The title 'Lord' is also used many times in the book of Amos in the Old Testament as God's name: 'Woe to you who desire the day of the LORD! Why would you have the day of the LORD? It is darkness, and not light...' (Amos 5:18). In the prophecy of Amos, it is clear that the LORD is an **omnipotent** ruler of all, to who all will answer at the end of time.

Useful vocabulary

Lord: a person who has power and authority; a title for God in the Old Testament, also used for Jesus in the New Testament

omnipotent: all powerful

How the title 'Lord' is used in the New Testament

'Lord' is used many times in the New Testament. Sometimes it is used to show someone who is a 'master' or who owns property. It is often used to refer to Jesus, showing that the disciples recognise him as their master. For the disciples then, it is a term of both recognition and respect. One example of this is in John's Gospel, in the story of Jesus appearing to seven disciples. This takes place after Jesus' crucifixion and resurrection when the disciples go fishing. Jesus stands on the shore speaking to the disciples, but they do not recognise him until a miracle occurs and they start to catch fish.

> " ‖ 'That disciple whom Jesus loved… said to Peter, "It is the Lord!"'
>
> *John 21:7*

There is an understanding then among all of the disciples that the person on the shore is Jesus; later the passage says: 'They knew it was the Lord' (John 21:12).

Elsewhere in the New Testament, such as in Paul's letters, the title is used to emphasise that Jesus is God. For example, when Paul says that at the end of time all people will bow the knee and confess that Jesus is Lord (Philippians 2:10), he is quoting from an Old Testament passage that uses this same phrase to refer to the authority of God (Isaiah 45:21–25).

Why do Christians refer to Jesus as 'Lord'?

For Christians today, 'Lord' is one of the most common ways of referring to Jesus, especially in prayer, where Jesus is addressed as 'Our Lord, Jesus Christ.' For Christians this is a way of acknowledging that Jesus is God and that he shares in God's authority and power. Addressing Jesus as 'Lord' recognises God's complete power over all, and that Jesus, as the Son of God, shares in this power. It is a way for Christians to show their acceptance of, and obedience to, God.

Son of God · · · · Messiah

Christ · · · · Son of Man

Lord · · · · Son of David

▲ *There are many titles for Jesus*

Understand

1 Why is the word 'LORD' written using all capitals in the Old Testament?

2 How did St Paul use the title 'Lord'?

3 How do the Gospel writers use the title 'Lord'?

4 Why do Christians today address Jesus as 'Lord'?

5 'Son of Man', 'Christ' and 'Lord' are titles which describe different things about who Jesus was. Explain these differences.

Discern

6 How would Christianity be different if Jesus was not believed to be God?

Respond

7 What does the claim 'Jesus is Lord' mean to you? Give reasons for your response.

WHAT IS THE TRINITY?

When the Catholic Church has an official teaching on a subject, it is referred to as a doctrine. These teachings are of special importance to the Catholic faith. The Holy Trinity is one such doctrine and its teaching that there is one God, who is at the same time three persons, is specific to Christianity. It is important to understand, however, that Christians are **monotheistic** and believe only in one God.

What is the doctrine of the Trinity?

The doctrine of the Trinity was defined by the early Church in the fourth century. 'Tri' comes from a Latin word for three. It is often used in the English language as a prefix for words which have something to do with the number three, for example triangle, which is a three-sided shape. In the case of the Trinity, it means the three divine persons of the Trinity: Father, Son and Holy Spirit. Each person of the Trinity is distinct from the others, each is fully God, and at the same time, there is only one God.

Because the Trinity is difficult for human beings to understand, it is referred to by the Church as a mystery – something that humans should not feel bad about finding difficult, because it reflects the ultimate mystery of God. The Catechism states:

> " 'The mystery of the Most Holy Trinity is the central mystery of Christian faith and life. It is the mystery of God in himself.'
>
> *Catechism of the Catholic Church 234*

Useful vocabulary

monotheistic: believing there is only one God

Link

Read more about the Incarnation on pages 68–69.

Who is God the Father?

God the Father is the first person of the Trinity. Catholics believe in 'God, the Father almighty, maker of heaven and earth' (Nicene Creed).

Who is God the Son?

Jesus is God the Son and the second person of the Trinity. Catholics believe that Jesus is truly divine and also truly human. God the Son came to Earth and lived among human beings. This is the belief of the Incarnation: that Jesus is God made flesh.

Who is God the Holy Spirit?

The Holy Spirit is the third person of the Trinity. Catholics believe that the Holy Spirit spoke through the prophets of the Old Testament and is present in the Church today. In the Bible, the Holy Spirit empowers the apostles in their mission to spread the Good News of Jesus during Pentecost.

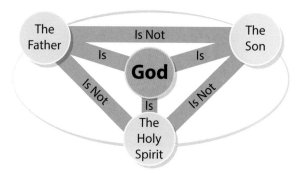

▲ *Using visual images can help people to understand the doctrine of the Trinity*

How can one God be three divine persons?

The doctrine of the Trinity is important because it explains how Jesus can be God incarnate, sent by the Father, without denying there is only one God.

The Trinity is not written about *directly* in the Bible. The Bible is clear that only one God exists: one of the Ten Commandants given to Moses was, 'You shall have no other gods before me' (Exodus 20:3). However, the presence of God as the Father, the Son and the Holy Spirit can be seen in the Bible:

- Jesus is often described as the 'Word of God', and is said to have been with God at the very beginning of time: 'In the beginning was the Word, and the Word was with God, and the Word was God' (John 1:1). At the Incarnation, this person of God then became flesh and lived on earth among humans.
- In the first verses of the Bible, the Holy Spirit is shown to be present at the creation of the world: 'And the Spirit of God was hovering over the face of the waters' (Genesis 1:2).

The Catholic Church believes Jesus helps Christians understand the Trinity. When Jesus gave his disciples their mission to share the Good News, he told them to do so in the name of all three persons of the Trinity:

> " 'Go therefore and make disciples of all nations, baptising them in the name of the Father and of the Son and of the Holy Spirit.'
>
> *Matthew 28:19*

Most importantly, Catholics believe that at Jesus' baptism all three persons of the Trinity were revealed. At his baptism, the Son is present in the person of Jesus, the Father's voice speaks from the heavens and the Spirit descends like a dove.

Together, these teachings formed the basis of the doctrine of the Trinity, which is a central belief of the Catholic Church today.

Understand

1 Why is the Trinity referred to as a 'doctrine'?
2 Where can the presence of the three persons of the Trinity be seen in the Bible?
3 What does it mean to describe the Trinity as a 'mystery'?
4 Look back at pages 68–69 about the Incarnation. How does understanding the doctrine of the Incarnation help you to understand the Christian belief in the Trinity?

Discern

5 Explain two pieces of evidence from the Bible that Catholics would use to support the idea of the Trinity.

Respond

6 The Church teaches that the Trinity is a mystery. Do you think it's possible to believe in something that you cannot fully understand?

HOW DOES CATHOLIC WORSHIP REFLECT BELIEF IN THE TRINITY?

As we read on pages 80–81, the Trinity is a very important part of Catholic belief. And as an important part of being a Christian is to worship God, the Trinity is at the heart of Catholic prayer, especially the Mass.

What does *lex orandi, lex credendi* mean?

The Catholic Church uses a special phrase to explain the connection between their worship and their beliefs. **Lex orandi, lex credendi** was first used by Prosper of Aquitane, a Christian writer in the fifth century. It means 'the law of prayer is the law of belief'. In other words, in Catholicism, worship and belief are completely intertwined. So, Catholic prayers underpin the beliefs of the Church and the beliefs of the Church (for example, belief in the Trinity) are reflected in how Catholics pray.

Therefore, worship and belief are a never-ending circle, strengthening one another and creating a faithful Church with the Trinity at its centre.

How is Catholic prayer always Trinitarian?

Catholic prayer is always Trinitarian (meaning it reflects the Trinity) because prayers are always offered to the Father, with and through the Son, by the power of the Holy Spirit. This is shown in the words of the prayers themselves, for example:

- The Sign of the Cross begins and ends all Catholic prayer and is a **devotion** to the Trinity. While making a cross shape using the right hand on the forehead, the middle of the chest, then the left and right shoulders, the following words are said: 'In the name of the Father, and of the Son and of the Holy Spirit'.
- The Sign of the Cross is also a prayer in itself and it is used frequently by Catholics, besides being used to start and end prayer. For example, Catholics might make the Sign of the Cross if a funeral procession passes them or before doing something that might be dangerous.
- Many formal prayers, such as the morning prayer of the Church, or the Rosary, use the Glory Be to mark the end of parts of the prayers. The Glory Be is a prayer of praise to the Trinity: 'Glory be to the Father, and to the Son, and to the Holy Spirit, as it was in the beginning, is now and ever shall be, world without end. Amen.'

Useful vocabulary

devotion: a religious practice which creates a feeling of love and commitment towards God

lex orandi, lex credendi: Latin phrase meaning 'the law of prayer is the law of belief'

▲ *The sign of the cross is made by touching the forehead, chest and shoulders*

The Trinity in the Mass

The whole Mass is an experience of God as the Trinity. In Mass, Catholics believe that the offering that Jesus made to the Father on the cross is made really present for them by the action of the Holy Spirit. The congregation's offering of bread and wine is transformed into the body and blood of Christ by the Holy Spirit. These are then offered in thanksgiving to the Father and shared with all those present during communion.

Link

Read more about the Mass on pages 56–57.

At Mass, the congregation express their beliefs by saying the Creed during the Liturgy of the Word. There are two creeds that Catholics use, but both refer to the most important beliefs that Catholics hold. The Nicene Creed is used most often and is structured around the three persons of the Trinity. It takes each person in turn and explains core beliefs around that person of the Trinity.

" I believe in one God, **the Father almighty**, maker of heaven and earth, of all things visible and invisible…

I believe in one **Lord Jesus Christ, the Only Begotten Son of God**, born of the Father before all ages…

I believe in **the Holy Spirit, the Lord**, the giver of life, who proceeds from the Father and the Son, who with the Father and the Son is adored and glorified, who has spoken through the prophets.

Nicene Creed

The Eucharistic prayer begins with a song of praise called the Sanctus (which is Latin for Holy). The Sanctus repeats the word 'holy' three times. This emphasises the divinity of God and reflects the Catholic belief in one God in three persons.

" **Holy, Holy, Holy** Lord God of hosts

The Eucharistic prayer ends with the 'Great Amen', where the congregation sing a final 'Amen' to all that has been prayed during the prayer. The priest introduces this Amen with a prayer that sums up the meaning of the Mass as an experience of the love of the Trinity. The reference to 'him' reminds the congregation that the Mass has been about the offering of Jesus, the Son of God who is really present in the Eucharist, to the Father, by the power of the Holy Spirit.

" **Through him, and with him, and in him**, O God, almighty Father, in the **unity** of the Holy Spirit, all glory and honour is yours, for ever and ever. **Amen.**

Understand

1 Explain what *lex orandi, lex credendi* means.

2 What is the Sign of the Cross?

3 Why is the Sign of the Cross important?

4 Describe two prayers of the Mass that refer to the persons of the Trinity.

5 Explain what a person might learn about the Trinity through the Nicene Creed.

6 How does the conclusion of the Eucharistic prayer show belief in the Trinity?

Discern

7 'Belief in the Trinity makes prayer confusing.' How far do you agree with this statement? How might a Catholic respond?

Link

Read more about how Jesus is present in the Eucharist on pages 106–107.

Respond

8 Do you pray? If so, who do you address your prayer to?

HOW IS JESUS THE PERFECT HUMAN BEING?

For Christians, the Incarnation meant that, for the first time, people could experience the real presence of God on earth. Catholics believe that Jesus is the perfect example to follow because he is God. They look to the Bible to learn from his actions and words, to be more faithful Christians and more humble people.

What does *Gaudium et Spes* teach?

Gaudium et Spes means 'Hope and Joy' and is a document from the Second Vatican Council held in 1965. It explores the way the Catholic Church should work in the whole world, not just for the good of Catholics, but for every human being. The way Jesus lived is used as an example of how Catholics everywhere should behave towards others:

> " 'He Who is "the image of the invisible God" (Col. 1:15), is Himself the perfect man… For by His incarnation the Son of God has united Himself in some fashion with every [human being]. He worked with human hands, He thought with a human mind, acted by human choice and loved with a human heart. Born of the Virgin Mary, He has truly been made one of us, like us in all things except sin.'
>
> *Gaudium et Spes 22*

This is a reminder of the Incarnation. As Jesus is God, then he cannot be anything but perfect, as God is **omnibenevolent**. God is goodness and so Jesus must be too.

Gaudium et Spes mentions all of the ways in which human beings can relate to Jesus; all of those human qualities that we possess, such as decision making, love, having a family. It is a reminder that even though Jesus is perfect, he is still a human being, and therefore Catholics can follow his example in the things they do in the world.

How is Jesus the 'perfect' human being?

In *Gaudium et Spes 22*, Jesus is described as 'the perfect man', but ordinary human beings are not perfect. Genesis 3 explains how Adam and Eve were banished from the Garden of Eden after they disobeyed God. This symbolic story about the origin of sin describes how sin broke the relationship of trust between God and all humanity, and has been inherited by every person since. *Gaudium et Spes* described humanity's relationship with God as 'disfigured from the first sin onward' (*Gaudium et Spes 22*). However, Jesus came to earth to fix this relationship and bring humanity back towards God. Through the Incarnation, Catholics believe the Word (Jesus) became flesh to be, among other things, a model of holiness for human beings to see. He did this in many ways, for example through his teachings and in the miracles that he performed. The main theme throughout all of Jesus' work is that of love and forgiveness. His message is about improving a person's soul and acting with a pure heart. This in itself shows Jesus' goodness: he wants humans to love one another and not to quarrel, fight or abuse each other.

Useful vocabulary

omnibenevolent: all loving

Link

Read more about the documents of the Second Vatican Council on pages 44–45 and 50–51.

Earlier we read about the request of James and John to be seated alongside Jesus in heaven. Jesus corrects their human misunderstandings about what his life on earth is about. He summarises this at the end of the passage: 'For even the Son of Man came not to be served but to serve, and to give his life as a ransom for many' (Mark 10:45). Jesus spent three years teaching about good ways to live, which all human beings can learn from. However, the most important way in which Jesus showed his perfection was through the ultimate sacrifice of his life. He endured immense physical and emotional pain during his crucifixion – a 'ransom' – to ensure the rest of humanity was saved. When Jesus did this, he demonstrated a pure and selfless love called agape.

What can Catholics learn from Jesus?

Catholics are called to be transformed into Jesus' likeness and the main way in which they can do this is by demonstrating agape. Catholic Social Teaching asks Catholics to serve others in their day-to-day lives through kind actions, forgiveness or selfless deeds. For some Catholics, this might extend to what career they choose. For example, some Catholics may go into the caring or medical professions in order to live out the Christian value of service to others.

The dignity of the human person is a core part of Catholic Social Teaching. Catholics believe that all human beings are special because we have all been made by God. Every person is equal in dignity and deserves to have their human rights defended. No matter how much money we have or where we are from or any of our differences, God loves us completely. Catholics believe we should follow God's example and show the same love to all of our fellow human beings.

Link

Read more about the Son of Man on pages 74–75.

▼ *While celebrating Mass on Holy Thursday at a prison in Rome, Pope Francis washes the feet of 12 inmates to represent the 12 apostles whose feet Jesus washed*

Link

Read more about Catholic Social Teaching on pages 24–25.

Understand

1 Identify two key phrases that a Catholic might learn from *Gaudium et Spes 22*.
2 Give two examples of how a Catholic might see Jesus' goodness.
3 What is agape? How and why did Jesus demonstrate this?
4 What does 'the dignity of the human person' mean?

Discern

5 Do you think a Catholic has a duty to serve others? Give two reasons for your response.
6 'A person cannot be truly human and without sin.' How would a Catholic respond to this view? Include a reference to *Gaudium et Spes* in your answer.
7 Do you think that society is respectful of the dignity of every human being? Give reasons for your answer.

Respond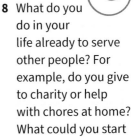

8 What do you do in your life already to serve other people? For example, do you give to charity or help with chores at home? What could you start to do to make sure that you are serving others?

CAN BUSINESSES ACT SELFLESSLY?

OBJECTIVES

In this lesson you will explore **how corporate social responsibility means businesses should be selfless rather than self-serving.**

Corporate social responsibility is the idea that organisations and businesses should operate in a way that benefits society as a whole rather than just making money for themselves. Many companies explain their 'business ethics' in mission statements which set out their goals and how they will achieve them in an **ethical** way. Does this mean these businesses are acting selflessly?

Why is corporate social responsibility important?

Corporate social responsibility is very important in today's world. As more and more businesses operate globally, rather than just in one country, the impact they have on the world has increased. Today's fast-paced communications mean we can quickly see this impact and companies can more easily be held accountable for their actions.

Many powerful businesses have been accused of acting selfishly by exploiting workers and producers in developing nations to give their customers cheap, plentiful goods. This behaviour, for example not paying a fair wage to workers, goes against the principle of the dignity of the human person from Catholic Social Teaching. The environment is also being damaged due to intensive farming and forest clearance, to satisfy global demands.

Increasingly, businesses choose to demonstrate corporate social responsibility and let customers know what their values are as a business and what they do to uphold those values. This can be written into their mission statement. For example, they might commit to taking care of the people who work for them, reducing their environmental impact, or helping support the local area in which they are based.

What is outwardly virtuous behaviour?

To be selfless is to act without thought for yourself, and in the best interests of other people. An example of selfless behaviour in the business world might be agreeing to pay a minimum wage to factory workers despite the fact it will reduce a company's profits. Actions which demonstrate high moral standards can be described as virtuous behaviour. Sometimes, a person or company's behaviour may appear to be ethical and selfless to the outside world (it is outwardly virtuous), but does that mean they always make decisions in the best interests of others?

For example, many people today prefer to buy products from companies that treat their workers well, or who show care for the environment. So a business might sell more of its products if it claims to do so.

Useful vocabulary

ethical: relating to moral principles or beliefs about what is right and wrong

sustainable: able to be kept going or maintained over time

Link

Read more about Catholic Social Teaching on pages 24–25.

What is 'greenwashing'?

It could be argued that there is nothing wrong with making more money while doing some good in the world. However, sometimes businesses are accused of using a small amount of ethical behaviour to distract people from their unethical behaviour. For example, 'greenwashing' is when a business gives the impression that they are working in a way that is **sustainable** and environmentally friendly, but in fact there is lots that they are doing that contradicts this. Several fashion brands have been criticised for this behaviour, which might include:

▲ We can make ethical choices as consumers when choosing who to give our money to

- Making a small collection of clothes which is advertised as 'sustainable' or 'eco' when the majority of the clothes they make are not.
- Saying they use 'sustainable materials' but not saying whether the rest of the production process is sustainable. For example, how much water is used during the process? How are the goods transported? Are all workers paid fairly and treated well?
- Describing the clothes they make in misleading ways, for example by saying clothes are made from recycled materials, when this may only make up a small percentage of the material used.

Many companies are motivated to show what they are doing to support sustainability because they know this is important to their customers. However, if they are only interested in how they can increase their profits, rather than having a positive impact on the world, then their behaviour is not selfless, but self-serving.

This does not follow the teaching that Catholics believe Jesus tried to share in the story of the Request of James and John (see pages 74–75) – that we should act selflessly in the service of others.

Understand

1 What is corporate social responsibility?
2 Give an example of ethical business behaviour.
3 What is self-serving behaviour?
4 Explain what 'greenwashing' is.

Discern

5 Do you think it matters if people act selflessly as long as their actions help others? Write a paragraph to explain your views.
6 'There is no such thing as a truly selfless act.' How far would you agree or disagree with this? How might a Catholic respond?

Respond

7 Think about the last week. What actions have you carried out that you think would have seemed virtuous to other people? For example, holding the door for someone, or helping make dinner. Do you think your actions were selfless or self-serving?

WHAT CAN CATHOLICS LEARN FROM RUBLEV'S *TRINITY?*

Many artists have created pieces of art to reflect the doctrine of the Trinity. Trinitarian art can help Christians to understand the complex idea of one God in three persons.

Andrei Rublev and iconography

Andrei Rublev was a Russian painter who lived from 1360 to 1430. His most famous work is an **icon** which has come to be known as *Trinity*. Icons are used in different **denominations** of Christianity, but especially in the Orthodox Church, a branch of Christianity found mainly in Eastern Europe and in parts of the Middle East. An icon is considered to be a sacred object by many Eastern Orthodox Christians because they believe it makes present in some way the person or event which it represents. The process of painting an icon is often a prayerful experience. There are usually many icons at the front of an Orthodox Church through which Christians may focus their prayers.

> **Useful vocabulary**
>
> **icon:** a religious image, particularly popular in Orthodox Christianity, used for devotion or worship

What is Rublev's *Trinity*?

Rublev's *Trinity* is an interpretation of the Old Testament story in Genesis 18:1–16, when Abraham and Sarah are visited by three men, whom Abraham recognises as God. Sarah is told she will have a son, but she does not believe it as she thinks she is unable to have children. A year later she gives birth to Isaac.

Rublev's icon brings together ideas that allow us to understand this as being an artwork, not just about God's appearance to Abraham, but God's appearance as the Trinity.

> In the centre there appears to be an altar with a chalice (cup) on top – a reminder of the Catholic and Orthodox Christian belief in the Eucharist and how this brings an individual closer to all three persons of the Trinity. There is also the head of a sacrificed animal in the chalice, thought to represent the sacrifice of Christ.

▲ Trinity *by Andrei Rublev*

Meg Wroe's *Trinity – After Rublev*

Meg Wroe decided to paint a different version of Rublev's Trinity. Her main reason for doing this was the lack of diversity in the art usually seen in churches. In Wroe's painting, the angels are ethnically diverse and are represented as two women and one man. The angels are based on friends of Wroe from St Luke's Church in West Holloway, London.

▲ Trinity – After Rublev *by Meg Wroe*

The three angels sit in a triangle and are all the same size. This suggests they are all equally important. The angels are not depicted as being obviously male or female.

All three bow their heads and have tranquil expressions which creates symmetry and a feeling of unity.

Gold makes the picture seem heavenly, for example the gold of the halos and the wings of the angels. It is a reminder of the glory and power of God.

It is thought that the colours of the robes give some insight as to who each of the angels represent:
- The robes of the angel on the left are almost transparent. This angel represents God the Father: invisible, yet always present.
- The angel on the right wears blue and green like the earth. This represents the Holy Spirit who is a presence during the creation stories in Genesis.
- The angel in the centre wears blue (which represents heaven) and brown (which represents earth). This angel is Jesus, (God the Son) who brings together both heaven and earth in his human and divine natures.

The angels are barefoot. In many cultures, taking off shoes is a mark of respect, suggesting that the ground the angels stand on is holy.

Understand

1 What is an icon?
2 Why are icons used by some Christians?
3 Describe two features of Rublev's icon which suggest it represents the Trinity.
4 Which person of the Trinity is represented by which angel?

Discern

5 Look at both artworks on these pages. What story do they tell? How are they similar and how are they different? Do you think they do a good job of showing Catholic beliefs about the Trinity?
6 'No artwork can really help us understand the mystery of the Trinity.' Do you agree with this statement? How might a Catholic respond to this?

Respond

7 Design your own artwork to depict the Trinity. Think about the ideas in Rublev and Wroe's artworks – what elements might you use? What would you do differently?

WHO WAS FATHER MYCHAL JUDGE?

Religious brothers and sisters sometimes live separately from the rest of society in closed monasteries, but they can also carry out their vows to serve God by living and working among others. Father (Fr) Mychal Judge **OFM** was a Franciscan **friar** who worked in New York City and gave his life in the service of others.

Who are the Franciscans?

The Franciscans are an order of religious brothers and sisters within the Catholic Church. The order was originally founded in 1209. Franciscans are inspired by St Francis of Assisi, whose personal qualities and beliefs have shaped the lives of Franciscans to the present day. Franciscans are described as mendicant, which means they take a vow of poverty and live very basic, simple lives with few material possessions. This allows them to focus on what they consider is more important in life: prayer, charity and humility. They try to enjoy God's creation in the natural world and focus on all of the good things we have to celebrate in our world.

▲ *St Francis of Assisi was an Italian Catholic friar and is the patron **saint** of animals*

Useful vocabulary

OFM: Orders of Friars Minor, an abbreviation used after the name of certain Franciscan friars to show which order they are from

friar: a religious brother who is a member of a mendicant order, for example Franciscans, Dominicans, Augustinians or Carmelites

saint: a person who is officially recognised by the Catholic Church as being very holy because of the way he or she lived, or died; also, anyone who is already in heaven, whether recognised or not

chaplain: a priest who is appointed to offer spiritual support to people in a particular organisation

Who was Fr Mychal Judge?

Fr Mychal Judge was a Franciscan priest who worked in the New York City Fire Department as a **chaplain**. As part of that role, he would offer encouragement and prayers at the sites of fires and during rescues. Later, Fr Mychal would visit the victims in hospital and support families in their times of distress and grief. He would often work long days, up to 16 hours. Aside from his work for the Fire Department, Fr Mychal also cared for the most vulnerable in the city. For example, once on a cold winter's evening, Fr Mychal took off his coat and gave it to a homeless woman who he passed, saying that she needed it more than him. Even before the events of 11 September 2001, Fr Mychal was known for living out the values of Jesus through his service to others.

Fr Mychal died on 11 September 2001. The date of Fr Mychal's death, known as 9/11, is recognised around the world because it is the date that terrorists hijacked four planes in the United States of America with the intention of crashing them into key buildings and killing as many people as possible. 2,977 people were killed. Fr Mychal Judge was the first victim recorded.

However, the high-profile cause of Fr Mychal's death meant his life's work was shared with many people, allowing his sacrifice to inspire others around the world. On 11 September, when hearing that New York's World Trade Center had been hit by two planes, he made his way straight there to offer his help. He entered the North Tower to help rescuers and the injured, and to pray over those who had died. When the South Tower collapsed, Fr Mychal was struck on the head by flying debris and was killed. A famous photo taken by Shannon Stapleton shows a police officer and four firefighters, to whom Fr Mychal was probably known, carrying his body out of the tower rubble. The love and respect that these people had for Fr Mychal is evident in the photograph and is a reminder of the huge sacrifice he made: giving his life while trying to help others.

▲ *Some people want Fr Mychal Judge to be made a saint in light of his life of sacrifice*

A model of Jesus' behaviour

A person who becomes a Franciscan intends to uphold many of the qualities that Jesus spoke of: sacrifice, service and respecting the dignity of every individual that God has created. Fr Mychal truly embraced the life of a Franciscan and was known for his prayerful life and service to others. Many Christians would feel there is no better way to model Jesus' behaviour than to devote a whole life to helping others.

Fr Mychal wrote a prayer that showed his trust in God and his willingness to act as a humble servant, just as Jesus did.

> "
> 'Lord, take me where You want me to go;
> Let me meet who You want me to meet;
> Tell me what You want me to say;
> And keep me out of Your way.'
>
> *Fr Mychal Judge, OFM*

Understand

1 Who are the Franciscans?
2 Give one way it might be difficult to be a Franciscan in our modern world.
3 Identify three facts about Fr Mychal Judge.
4 Why did Fr Mychal become very well known?
5 Describe the prayer that Fr Mychal wrote; what is its main theme?

Discern

6 Consider how strongly Fr Mychal's actions resemble those of Jesus.
7 Do you think Fr Mychal demonstrated some of the qualities that you would expect a saint to have? Explain your ideas.

Respond

8 How might Catholics support the work of the Franciscans today? Consider prayer and other means of physically supporting this religious order.

ASSESSMENT

Key vocabulary

Write a definition for these key terms.

Incarnation	Trinity	Son of Man	Son of God
Christ	Lord	heresy	Arianism
lex orandi, lex credendi	service		

Knowledge check

1   Which phrase best describes the Incarnation:

   a   Jesus is similar to God but mostly he is human.

   b   Jesus is both truly God and truly human.

   c   Sometimes Jesus is God, and sometimes he is human.

2   What important Christian festival is associated with the Incarnation?

3   Copy out and complete the following sentence:

   In the fourth century, Arius put forward the belief that Jesus was not ....

4   In what Church document is Jesus described as the 'perfect human being'?

5   Recall a phrase from the Nicene Creed which refers to Jesus.

6   Summarise the Catholic belief in the Trinity.

7   Identify two ways that the Trinity is referred to during the Mass.

8   Explain how the doctrines of the Trinity and the Incarnation are linked.

9   Describe what the 'Son of Man' title reveals about Jesus.

10 Explain why Jesus is 'Lord' for Christians.

TIP

Consider what the Bible says about the title 'Son of Man'. Look back at pages 74–75 to help you.

Extended writing activity

This assessment is for you to show what you have learned in this chapter and to develop your extended writing skills. Here is a big question:

> **Throughout the Bible Jesus is referred to by many different titles. Pick two of those titles and explain what they tell us about Jesus. Why do you think he was known by so many different names?**

This can be broken down into two smaller parts. Your teacher will direct you to which parts they want you to answer.

1 **Pick one title. Explain what it tells us about Jesus.**

Write at least one paragraph to answer this part of the question. You should explain how the title relates to the Bible and why this is important. Here is an example of how you might begin:

> *Jesus is called by many different titles in the Bible: 'Son of God', 'Son of Man', 'Lord' and 'Christ'. The title 'Son of God' relates to two key Catholic doctrines – the Trinity and the Incarnation. The Old Testament tells of how the Jewish people had been waiting for a Messiah. A prophecy in Psalms says that God will refer to the Messiah as 'Son'. Christians believe that Jesus was this Messiah which then also reinforces the belief that Jesus is the Son of God, an essential person of the Trinity.*

Pick another title. Explain what it tells us about Jesus.

Write at least one paragraph answering this part of the question. You might find these sentence starters helpful.

> *Another title used to address Jesus is...*
>
> *The title... links to the Bible because...*
>
> *This is important because...*
>
> *It helps Christians to understand Jesus more because...*

Words you could use:

Christ   Lord   Son of Man   authority   doctrine

2 **Why do you think Jesus was known by so many different titles?**

Try to write at least one paragraph answering this question, giving reasons for your answer.

Words you could use:

belief   person   godliness   human   qualities

TIP

- *Remember, you must explain what the title tells us about Jesus, not just what the title means.*

- *Really good answers will provide lots of detail about the title being used. This might include a teaching that links directly to the title.*

1 This sentence describes how the title 'Son of God' is connected to two core Christian beliefs.

2 This sentence shows how the title 'Son of God' is connected to an Old Testament prophecy.

3 Next, you could write another paragraph to explain how the title 'Son of God' links to the Incarnation. This might begin 'For Christians, the Incarnation means...'

TIP

Think about why Jesus was referred to by these titles. You should try to include your own view in this paragraph with some reasons to support your point.

DESERT TO GARDEN

Introduction

Sometimes it can be hard to explain why things happen because an answer is complicated. **Sometimes we just can't explain events because they are beyond human understanding: they are a genuine mystery.**

The Paschal Mystery is one example you will study in this chapter: it is the mystery of how Jesus' death and resurrection was able to bring salvation to the world, and how Jesus is able to remain present in our world to this day through the body of the Church.

Through the Church, Catholics can receive sacraments, which give them the spiritual strength they need to live a good and selfless life, as Jesus did. At the heart of Catholic life lies the weekly celebration of the most important sacrament – the Sacrament of the Eucharist.

The Catholic Church teaches that **the Eucharist is the 'source and summit of the Christian life'** (CCC 1324). This ancient practice, that comes from the Last Supper, is so significant for Catholics that they have many names for it: the Holy Mass, Holy Communion, the Breaking of Bread, the Lord's Supper. Each name reveals something unique about the nature and importance of this sacrament.

The origins of the sacrament at the Last Supper have a deep connection to the traditional Jewish Passover meal. We have seen that many things

Jesus did fulfilled prophecies and promises made in the Old Testament. In this chapter we will see how, in Exodus, **the events of Passover foreshadow the final meal and sacrifice Jesus will make**.

We will learn what Catholics believe about the Eucharist and investigate what it means to experience the Real Presence of Jesus Christ in the Mass. Catholics believe that through the Eucharist, they can share in Jesus' sacrifice on the cross, which allows them to make a special connection with God. In this way **Jesus remains present in the life of the Church today, uniting Catholics with God and with each other**.

The Sacrament of the Eucharist is so central to the Catholic faith, **it touches every aspect of Catholic life and is not limited to worship at Mass.** The Eucharist is celebrated through special feasts and processions, and is an inspiration for great Catholic art.

The Catholic Church teaches that the Sacrament of the Eucharist is the greatest gift of all, allowing people today to connect with God in a profound way. It binds Catholics into one Christian body and, **united by this shared sacrament, Catholics believe they will be saved from the desert through salvation and enter the garden of everlasting life with God.**

OBJECTIVES

In this lesson you will explore **what is meant by the Paschal Mystery.**

WHAT IS THE PASCHAL MYSTERY?

The **Paschal Mystery** is the belief that Jesus' death and **resurrection** brought every human being freedom from sin and a way to eternal life with God. This is the most important message of Christianity, but how does God share this message with the world?

Good News about what?

In Chapter 2 we learned that the four Gospels are the central part of the New Testament. We also learned that Gospel means 'Good News' – but good news about what? Although there are many good things that the Catholic Church teaches to the world, there is one key message at the centre of it all: Jesus' death and resurrection was part of God's plan to save human beings from sin and evil. This is the Good News of Jesus' death and resurrection.

As such, Catholics believe that Jesus' death was not a cruel accident, but a great sacrifice made by God out of love for human beings. Furthermore, Jesus' sacrifice on the cross is then followed by his resurrection – Jesus who was truly dead comes back to life. Catholics believe that his resurrection offers the chance of eternal life with God in heaven for everyone: this is salvation. The Catholic Church teaches that Jesus' death and resurrection show the key message of Christianity and together these events are known as the Paschal Mystery.

> " ‖ 'The Paschal mystery of Christ's cross and Resurrection stands at the centre of the Good News that the apostles, and the Church following them, are to proclaim to the world.'
>
> *Catechism of the Catholic Church 571*

Useful vocabulary

Paschal Mystery: the belief that Jesus' death and resurrection bring salvation to every human being

resurrection: the Christian belief that after his crucifixion and death, Jesus rose back to life

Passover: a Jewish festival that celebrates God saving the Jewish people from slavery in Egypt

Link

Read more about Passover on pages 100–101.

What is the Paschal Mystery?

The 'Paschal' in Paschal Mystery refers back to the Jewish celebration of **Passover** (or *Pesach*) when Jewish people celebrate God's actions to free them from slavery in Egypt. Similarly, Jesus' actions free people from the slavery of sin and death. It is a mystery because it is an act of God and as such, is always beyond full human understanding, but by God's grace and through prayer, Catholics believe they can continually grow in their understanding of this mystery.

▲ *Catholics believe that Jesus' death and resurrection brings salvation for all people: this is the Paschal Mystery*

By the term 'Paschal Mystery' the Catholic Church means three things:
- The **actual events** of Jesus' arrest, trial, death on the cross and resurrection from the dead.
- The **significance of those events** for human beings: that Jesus' death on the cross frees human beings from sin, and that his resurrection opens the way to a new life with God.
- The idea that Jesus' death and resurrection are **made present** in the life of the Church today and can be experienced by Catholics – most directly in the celebration of the Mass and in the seven **sacraments**.

What does it mean to 'make present' the Paschal Mystery?

The Catholic Church teaches that, although Jesus' sacrifice and resurrection may be mysterious and hard to understand, they can be experienced even today. To be made present means more than just remembering these events – it means to take part in them. Catholics believe that the presence of the Holy Spirit on earth connects them to God and to Jesus. Jesus' death and resurrection are therefore present to Christians today through this spiritual connection in the following ways:
- First, in the seven sacraments: these are special rituals instituted by Jesus which Catholics can take part in, that are visible signs of God's **grace**.
- Secondly, in the liturgy, when Catholics gather together to worship God and experience God's **Real Presence** in the most important of the seven sacraments, the **Eucharist**.

The Catholic Church teaches that the sacraments and the liturgy are effective signs of God's salvation in the world today. Catholics believe that during these events God's love for them and for the world can be seen and felt. Liturgy and the sacraments help those who take part in them to receive God's grace. Grace is a special gift of love from God in which humans are forgiven for their sins and given strength to live as Christians. Just like medicine can help fight illness, so liturgy and the sacraments (for believers who receive them) cleanse them of sin and support them on the path to salvation.

Link

Read more about salvation on pages 48–49.

Useful vocabulary

sacraments: visible signs of God's grace that make real what they symbolise; also the name given to the ceremonies that contain these signs

grace: a gift of love freely given by God to humankind

Real Presence: the belief that Jesus is really present in the celebration of the Eucharist, in which the bread and wine truly become his body and blood

Eucharist: the sacrament in which Catholics receive the body and blood of Christ; also called Holy Communion, the Lord's Supper, the Breaking of the Bread and Mass

Understand

1 What are the key events of Jesus' life that are known as the Paschal Mystery?

2 What do Catholics believe is the importance of these key events in Jesus' life?

3 Explain two ways in which the Paschal Mystery is made present today, according to Catholic teaching.

Discern

4 'A religion should have one central message that is more important than anything else that it has to say to the world.' Do you agree? Give reasons for your answer.

Respond

5 What does the belief that Jesus is truly present in the Eucharist mean to you?

WHAT ARE THE SACRAMENTS OF THE CHURCH?

In Chapter 2 you learned about the three sources of authority for the Catholic Church, which included Apostolic Tradition. As the apostles established the early Church, they passed on what they were taught by Jesus, which included the celebration of the sacraments. A sacrament is a sacred **rite** which makes God's invisible, saving power visible and present to those who receive it. Through the Church, Catholics can receive seven sacraments, which are at the centre of religious life because they make the presence of Jesus in the world accessible to believers.

What is a sacrament?

St Augustine, an important bishop and thinker in the fourth century, called sacraments 'the visible form of an invisible grace' or 'a sign of a sacred thing'. A sacrament is therefore a religious ceremony using signs and symbols that humans can physically see, however, something special takes place during the ceremony that is *unseen*. This unseen part is grace – a special gift of love from God. It is through the visible signs themselves that this invisible grace becomes effective. Through the sacraments, God communicates and shares his love with human beings. Every time a Catholic receives a sacrament, they are transformed by this grace and their faith is nourished and strengthened.

What are the seven sacraments of the Catholic Church?

There are seven sacraments that a Catholic might receive. It is not necessary to receive all of them and some of them can be taken part in more than once.

Useful vocabulary

rite: a sacred act or ceremony

initiation: a ceremony to welcome or accept someone into an organisation

Holy Communion: another name for the Sacrament of Eucharist

vows: solemn promises which cannot be broken

Sacraments of Initiation:

There are three Sacraments of **Initiation**. It is important for a Catholic to receive all three to become a full member of the Church.

The Sacrament of Baptism: This is always the very first sacrament to be received. During Baptism, a person has water poured over their head, or they are fully immersed in a pool of water, three times (in the name of the Father, and of the Son, and of the Holy Spirit) as a sign of the washing away of sins and new birth in Christ that the sacrament brings about.

The Sacrament of Confirmation: Confirmation completes Baptism, and through it the Holy Spirit strengthens the gifts the person received at Baptism to prepare them to be a faithful, mature disciple. The bishop lays his hands on the person's head and anoints them with the oil of chrism.

The Sacrament of Eucharist: *Also called* **Holy Communion**. This sacrament is one that a Catholic will receive many times in their life. Catholics believe that during this sacrament the gifts of bread and wine are transformed into the body and blood of Christ, which are then eaten and drunk by those who receive Holy Communion. The first time a child receives the sacrament (usually around age 7), it is called First Holy Communion and is considered a special event.

Sacraments of Healing:

There are two Sacraments of Healing. Each of these can be received more than once.

The Sacrament of Reconciliation: Sometimes called Confession or the Sacrament of Penance, this sacrament helps a person prepare for receiving the Eucharist and ultimately receiving Jesus into their lives. It is a sacrament that a Catholic can receive as often as they wish and it is an opportunity to confess their sins to God, with the priest there to assist in this, and to receive forgiveness.

The Sacrament of the Anointing of the Sick: This sacrament is given when a Catholic is ill or dying in order to bring spiritual and physical strength to that person. See pages 92–93.

Sacraments at the Service of Communion:

There are two vocational sacraments which some Catholics are called to receive, but not all.

The Sacrament of Holy Orders: When receiving this sacrament, a man will make **vows** to devote his life to the service of God as a priest, deacon or bishop. The sacrament is given when the bishop lays his hands on the candidate and asks the Holy Spirit to consecrate for the ministry he is about to begin.

The Sacrament of Matrimony: During the ceremony of a Catholic marriage, the man and woman make vows to love and care for each other as husband and wife until the end of their lives. They will exchange rings which symbolise that there is no end to a Catholic marriage.

Why are sacraments important to Catholics?

Each sacrament strengthens a Catholic person's journey of faith at whatever stage they might be, because Catholics believe that the sacraments allow them to experience the healing, forgiving, nourishing, strengthening presence of God at every stage of their life. Many of the sacraments are directly rooted in the Gospel stories of Jesus. For instance, during the Sacrament of Baptism, Catholics believe they are directly following in the Great Commission of Jesus, who before ascending to heaven, commanded his disciples to baptise all the nations of the world in the name of the Father, Son and Holy Spirit.

> **"**
> 'Christ instituted the sacraments of the new law. The seven sacraments touch all of the stages and all of the important moments of Christian life.'
>
> *Catechism of the Catholic Church 1210*

Understand

1 What is a sacrament?

2 Identify the three Sacraments of Initiation.

3 Describe the two Sacraments of Healing.

4 What type of sacrament is the Sacrament of Matrimony?

5 Which sacrament can only be undertaken by a man?

6 How is Jesus connected to the seven sacraments?

Discern

7 'Jesus is an idea, not a real person for Christians today.' How might a Catholic respond to this statement? Refer to the sacraments in your answer.

Respond

8 Are there any rites, ceremonies or events that you feel help you grow in your faith or as a person?

WHY WAS THE LAST SUPPER SO IMPORTANT?

The Last Supper was a meal that Jesus shared with his disciples on the night before his death, to celebrate the Jewish Passover. Catholics remember the Last Supper every time they go to Mass.

Why was Jesus having a meal with his disciples?

Jesus was Jewish and so he celebrated Jewish festivals. Every spring, Jews celebrate Passover which commemorates God saving the Jewish people from slavery in Egypt. While they were enslaved, it was difficult for the Jewish people to worship because their spirits were broken. In the story of Passover, God called Moses to ask Pharaoh to set the Jewish people free so they could worship God, but Pharaoh refused and so God sent a series of ten plagues to try to change his mind. The last of these plagues was a terrible one: 'For I will pass through the land of Egypt that night, and I will strike all the firstborn… both man and beast' (Exodus 12:12).

The only way to avoid this was to follow the instructions given by God. In Exodus 12:1–14, God gives instructions to Moses and Aaron (Moses' brother) about the final meal that the Jewish people were to eat in Egypt. This became the first Passover meal. They were told to:
- Sacrifice a lamb and put some of its blood on the door frame of the house.
- Roast the flesh of the lamb and eat it with unleavened bread and bitter herbs.
- Eat the meal quickly and be ready to leave, dressed and wearing sandals.

The blood on the door frame was a sign to the angel of death to pass over the houses of the families who had followed God's instructions. This protected the Jewish children, but the first-born children of the Egyptians died. Pharaoh's son died and, in his grief and anger, he sent the Jewish people out of Egypt – God's plan had worked.

At Passover, Jews celebrate God's faithfulness and commit to strengthening their relationship with God by following the Mitzvot (commandments). They have a special meal with symbolic foods which remind them of the bitter slavery in Egypt and the joy of freedom.

▼ The Last Supper *by Lorna May Wadsworth; the Last Supper was a meal that Jesus shared with his disciples the night before he died, to celebrate the Jewish Passover*

Jesus' Last Supper

Luke's Gospel describes Jesus' words and actions at the Last Supper:

> " '... he took a cup, and when he had given thanks he said, "Take this, and divide it among yourselves. For I tell you that from now on I will not drink of the fruit of the vine until the kingdom of God comes." And he took bread, and when he had given thanks, he broke it and gave it to them, saying, "This is my body, which is given for you. Do this in remembrance of me." And likewise the cup after they had eaten, saying, "This cup that is poured out for you is the new covenant of my blood." '
>
> *Luke 22:17–20*

Two main features of the Passover meal were bread and wine. The bread was to remember the unleavened bread eaten that night in Egypt and the wine to celebrate freedom. Jesus took the bread and wine, blessed them and said of the bread 'This is my body' and of the wine 'This is my blood' (Matthew 26:28). Catholics believe that when he says this he is speaking about the sacrifice of himself on the cross to save humans from their sin. This is important for three reasons:

- The Jewish people sacrificed a lamb to save their first-born boys and Jesus is the Lamb of God, who would be sacrificed to save humankind.
- The Jewish people were freed from slavery and Jesus' sacrifice would free humankind from sin.
- Jesus' death was a sign of God's never-ending love and commitment to humans.

The Church teaches that the connections between the Passover described in the Old Testament, and the actions of Jesus at the Last Supper are not a coincidence. Catholics believe that the Passover foreshadows the sacrifice that Jesus will make in the future. Foreshadowing is the suggestion that some event happening now is a sign of an important event that will happen in the future. There are other places in the Old Testament where actual prophecies or predictions take place, and Jesus is seen to fulfil these prophecies too.

The Youth Catechism explains the connection between the Old Testament and the New Testament that can be found in Jesus: 'The entire Old Testament prepares for the Incarnation of God's Son. All of God's promises find their fulfilment in Jesus' (YC 18).

What does this mean for Catholics today?

The Catechism says that when Jesus celebrated the Last Supper he 'gave the Jewish Passover its definitive meaning' (CCC 1340). This is because Passover shows that God wanted to free people who were enslaved and Catholics believe that the greatest way in which God did this was through Jesus dying to free humans from being slaves to sin.

Catholics look forward to being in God's Kingdom, where they believe that they will have the 'final Passover' – they will be completely free because they will be living in God's love in a Kingdom far better than this world.

Understand

1 What is Passover?

2 Describe the instructions for the first Passover meal.

3 Describe what happened at the Last Supper which Catholics continue in the Eucharist today.

4 Write down at least two ways in which Passover and the Last Supper are connected.

5 Why do Catholics believe that the Last Supper gives Passover 'definitive meaning'?

Discern

6 'It is important to know about the Passover before you can properly understand the Mass.' Do you agree with this statement? Give reasons for your answer.

Respond

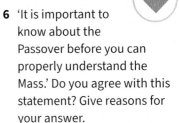

7 Catholics believe that Jesus sacrificed himself to save humankind. What does this mean to you?

WHAT IS THE EUCHARIST?

The Sacrament of the Eucharist is the central sacrament of the Catholic Church. In this sacrament Catholics are able to experience Christ's saving love, and be united to each other in celebrating it.

The Sacrament of the Eucharist

The Catholic Church teaches that Jesus gave the Church the seven sacraments as a way to share his love and grace with all people of the world. The sacraments are described as a visible sign of God's grace, that allow Catholics today to experience the saving power of the Paschal Mystery. Catholics believe that when they take part in the sacraments, the power of Christ's death and resurrection is made real for them. Through the sacraments they also become united more closely to each other in Christ's body, the Church.

The Eucharist is the most important of all the sacraments of the Church and is one of the Sacraments of Initiation. It is the final Sacrament of Initiation and through it the person becomes fully initiated into the Church. During the Eucharist, Catholics obey Christ's instruction to 'Do this in remembrance of me'. They believe that in the Eucharist the bread and wine are transformed into the body and blood of Christ. When Catholics take part in the Eucharist, they are present at the Last Supper of Christ with his apostles. In celebrating the sacred meal, the power of Christ's sacrificial offering of himself becomes really present to those who receive it. Catholics also believe that:

- By receiving the body and blood, they each become a part of Jesus' body: a personal connection.
- By sharing the body and blood, Catholics become part of one another: a community.
- Thus the Church becomes what it receives: the **Body of Christ**.

Catholics regularly take part in the Eucharist to unite themselves to the sacrifice of Christ on the cross and to join the community of the Church in offering thanks.

Useful vocabulary

Body of Christ: one of the names of the Church, emphasising the community of all those who are members of Christ's body through baptism, with Jesus as their head, working together like one body

Link

Read more about the seven sacraments on pages 98–99 and the Pascal Mystery on pages 96–97.

What does the 'source and summit' of the Christian life mean?

The Catholic Church teaches that the Sacrament of the Eucharist is its most important sacrament.

" 'The Eucharist is "**the source and summit of the Christian life**".'

Catechism of the Catholic Church 1324

The 'source of the Christian life' means it unites all Catholics into one Church with Christ. This then offers them grace, which is essential to live a Christian life. Grace provides spiritual strength both to live life day-to-day, and to carry the message of Jesus' love to others.

The 'summit of the Christian life' means it is the greatest gift offered by Christ to the Church. Catholics believe that at the end of life they will join the heavenly banquet and that the Eucharist here on earth is a taste of that banquet to come.

Why is the Eucharist seen as the most important sacrament?

The Catechism of the Catholic Church calls the Eucharist 'the Sacrament of sacraments' (CCC 1330). This means that all the other sacraments, and in fact all forms of Catholic worship, revolve around the Sacrament of the Eucharist.

All sacraments are valuable for Catholics because they make the saving power of Christ's death and resurrection present for believers. However, the Eucharist makes Jesus himself visible in the Real Presence. In the Eucharist, Catholics believe that human beings come as close to God as is possible on earth. In the Eucharist, Catholics believe they are gathering at the foot of the cross as Jesus offers himself in love to the Father. This event is made present for them during the Mass.

Therefore, the Eucharist is the most important of the sacraments and the most important form of Catholic worship because:

- it is the sacrament where Jesus is really present
- all the other sacraments direct a person towards the Eucharist, for example the Sacrament of Reconciliation prepares a Catholic to be worthy of receiving of the body of Christ
- the Eucharist is the centre of Church worship and life. Everything within the Church revolves around the celebration of the Eucharist. Even the design of a church building positions the altar, where the Eucharistic offering is made, at the centre
- the Eucharist connects all Catholics, uniting them with God and with each other.

Link

Read more about how Jesus is really present in the Eucharist on pages 106–107.

Understand

1 What type of sacrament is the Eucharist?
2 Explain what the Body of Christ is.
3 What does it mean to describe the Eucharist as the source of Christian life?
4 What does it mean to describe the Eucharist as the summit of Christian life?

Discern

5 Imagine you have to explain what the Sacrament of the Eucharist is to somebody who has never heard of it. Which part of the sacrament would you focus on to explain it and why?

Respond

6 What gives you strength in your daily life? How does this help you now and how do you think this will help you in the future?

WHY ARE THERE MANY NAMES FOR THE EUCHARIST?

The Sacrament of the Eucharist is rich with meaning. It helps Catholics to be faithful Christians in more than one way. As a result of this, the Eucharist is known by several names, including Mass and Holy Communion, and each name shows an important side of this central part of Catholic worship.

Why is the sacrament called the Eucharist?

> 'It is called… Eucharist, because it is an action of **thanksgiving to God**.'
>
> *Catechism of the Catholic Church 1328*

The word Eucharist literally means 'thanksgiving'. In this sacrament, Catholics give thanks to God for all that was done for them: the creation of the world, the opportunity to live holy lives and, most importantly, the sacrifice of Christ on the cross, so that all people of the world can be saved from sin.

The different names of the Eucharist

In the Sacrament of the Eucharist, Catholics have an opportunity to join together as a community to experience God's love and friendship. This rich experience is so significant for Catholics that it is known under many names, each showing something different about the sacrament and why it is celebrated.

Useful terms

Lord's Supper: another name for the Sacrament of Eucharist

The Lord's Supper brings Catholics to share at the table of Jesus' Last Supper.

Effect: Catholics believe that sharing the **Lord's Supper** with Jesus offers a first experience of the joy of heaven that awaits them in the future.

> 'The Lord's Supper, because of its connection with the supper which the Lord took with his disciples on the eve of his Passion and because it anticipates the wedding feast of the Lamb in the heavenly Jerusalem.'
>
> *Catechism of the Catholic Church 1329*

The Breaking of Bread was used by the early Christians to refer to the Eucharist. After his resurrection, Jesus' disciples were able to recognise Jesus when he broke bread with them and shared a meal.

Effect: Christians today recognise Jesus in one another when they break bread together and they recognise that Christ is really present with them in this sacrament.

> 'The Breaking of Bread, because Jesus used this rite…, when as master of the table he blessed and distributed the bread… It is by this action that his disciples will recognise him after his Resurrection'
>
> *Catechism of the Catholic Church 1329*

Holy Communion is a reminder that in this sacrament, Catholics are joined together as one Church community, and joined with God.

Effect: By receiving the sacrament, Catholics have the opportunity to celebrate the great gift that is the Church.

> 'Holy Communion, because by this sacrament we unite ourselves to Christ, who makes us sharers in his Body and Blood to form a single body.'
> *Catechism of the Catholic Church 1331*

Mass comes from the Latin word *missio* meaning 'mission'.

Effect: It shows that when Catholics receive this sacrament, they also receive a mission from God. They are called to take the grace that they receive through the sacrament out into the world – a mission which shares the love and kindness of God, and the saving power of Christ's death and resurrection, with others.

> 'Holy Mass (Missa), because the liturgy... concludes with the sending forth (missio) of the faithful, so that they may fulfil God's will in their daily lives.'
> *Catechism of the Catholic Church 1332*

What do the names for the Eucharist mean for Catholics?

The Eucharist has been the central form of worship in Christianity from the very beginning. Over time Catholics have come to understand the layers of meaning which are shown by the many different names given to the sacrament:

> 'The inexhaustible richness of this sacrament is expressed in the different names we give it. Each name evokes certain aspects of it.'
> *Catechism of the Catholic Church 1328*

The Catholic Church teaches that each name reveals something new and different about the Eucharist. It is such a meaningful ritual that each name can only explain a small part of what the Eucharist is and what it means for Catholics. Each name contributes one part to a greater understanding of the whole sacrament.

▲ Supper at Emmaus *by Matthias Stom; in the story of the Road to Emmaus, two disciples meet Jesus on the road and invite him to join them; they do not recognise him as Jesus until the breaking of the bread*

Understand

1 What does the word 'Eucharist' mean?
2 What does the name 'Breaking of Bread' mean for Catholics?
3 What do Catholics experience in the Lord's Supper?
4 Explain what the name 'Mass' teaches Catholics to do.
5 Explain why there is more than one name for the Eucharist.

Discern

6 Which name do you think best shows what the Eucharist means? Give reasons for your answer.

Respond

7 Which of the names of the Sacrament of the Eucharist mean the most to you?

HOW IS JESUS PRESENT IN THE EUCHARIST?

OBJECTIVES

*In this lesson you will learn **how Jesus is present in the Sacrament of the Eucharist.***

As we have read, the Catholic Church teaches that the Sacrament of the Eucharist is the 'source and summit of the Christian life.' This means that celebrating the Eucharist in the Mass is the most important form of worship for all Catholics. One of the most significant reasons for this is that, in the Sacrament of the Eucharist, Christians experience the Real Presence of Jesus.

How is Jesus present in the celebration of the Mass?

The Church teaches that even though Jesus ascended into heaven after his resurrection, he continues to be present among Christians, especially in the celebration of the Eucharist during Mass.

> " 'To accomplish so great a work, Christ is always present in His Church, especially in [the Church's] liturgical celebrations.'
>
> *Sacrosanctum Concilium 7*

Catholics believe that Jesus is present in the Mass in four ways:

In the assembly of the faithful:
Jesus is present when Christians gather together. The Bible says: 'For where two or three are gathered in my name, there am I among them' (Matthew 18:20). This is why one of the names for the Church is the Body of Christ.

In the reading of the scripture:
Jesus is present in the Liturgy of the Word, and particularly in the proclamation of the Gospel when Catholics hear about what he did and actually hear his words spoken directly to them.

Useful vocabulary

in persona Christi: Latin phrase for 'in the person of Christ'; the priest stands in the place of Jesus, who speaks through him during the Mass

Blessed Sacrament: a term that refers to the body and blood of Jesus in the Eucharist

consecrated: blessed and made holy

transubstantiation: the process by which the bread and wine actually become the body and blood of Jesus at the moment of consecration

In the priest:

During the Mass, the priest stands *in persona Christi* which is a Latin phrase for 'in the person of Christ'. This means that Jesus speaks through him when the priest says the words 'This is my body... this is my blood.'

In the Blessed Sacrament:

Most importantly, Catholics believe that in the Sacrament of the Eucharist they can experience the 'real presence' of Jesus. This means they believe that when the bread and wine are consecrated, they really become Jesus' body and blood, and therefore he is wholly and entirely present to the congregation. As the Bible teaches in the story of the Road to Emmaus: 'he was known to them in the breaking of the bread' (Luke 24:35).

The essential signs of the Eucharist

There are two essential signs of the Eucharist that Catholics can see: the bread and the wine. The Catechism explains that during the Sacrament of the Eucharist, the bread and wine truly become Jesus' body and blood, so they are more than just symbols:

> 'there takes place a change of the whole substance of the bread into the substance of the body of Christ our Lord and of the whole substance of the wine into the substance of his blood.'
>
> *Catechism of the Catholic Church 1376*

The change from the bread and wine into the body and blood of Jesus is known as **transubstantiation** and this takes place after the priest speaks the words of consecration ('This is my body... this is my blood'). Catholics believe the bread and wine are miraculously changed at this moment.

Some Christians do not believe Jesus is actually present in the bread and wine; for them the bread and wine simply represent Jesus' body and blood. Catholics, however, do not agree that the Blessed Sacrament is a symbol of Jesus. They believe that Jesus is invisibly but actually there.

What are the effects of the Eucharist?

The Catholic Church teaches that receiving the Eucharist gives Catholics:

- a personal connection with God
- a stronger faith
- forgiveness for sins
- protection from sins in the future
- a closer relationship with other Catholics which makes the whole Church stronger
- a commitment to serve the poor, as Jesus did.

Understand

1 Outline the four ways Jesus is present during the Mass according to the Catholic Church.

2 Why do Catholics say that Jesus is really present in the Blessed Sacrament?

3 What do Catholics mean by the term 'transubstantiation'?

4 Give three effects of receiving the body and blood of Jesus.

Discern

5 'The Real Presence of Jesus is the most significant aspect of the Eucharist'. Do you agree with this statement? Give reasons for your answer.

Respond

6 Do you believe that during Mass the bread and wine become the real body and blood of Jesus? What does the Blessed Sacrament mean to you?

WHY IS THE MASS CALLED A SACRIFICE?

Making a sacrifice means giving up something that is of value to you for the sake of something or someone else. The celebration of the Catholic Mass is sometimes called the 'The Holy **Sacrifice of the Mass**'. But why is it called a sacrifice? Who is sacrificed and why? In this lesson you will consider the connections between Jesus' actions at the Last Supper and the events of Passover, and the important part that sacrifice plays in both.

What does it mean that Jesus is the 'Lamb of God'?

During the Last Supper, Jesus and his disciples celebrated the Jewish festival of Passover, an important memorial that allows Jewish people to re-live the time when God saved the Jewish people from slavery in Egypt, as told in Exodus 12:21–26. During Passover celebrations in Jesus' time, Jewish families would travel to Jerusalem to each offer a lamb as a sacrifice to God in the Temple of Jerusalem, and afterwards gather together for a meal where they ate the meat of the lamb. This was a reminder of the sacrifice and blood of the original lamb of the Passover which protected them from the angel of death.

Jesus chose the Passover celebration to speak to his disciples, and chose his words very carefully. To Catholics this means that Jesus revealed himself to be the true Passover lamb. Here are some reasons why Catholics believe this:

Link

Read more about the Jewish festival of Passover and how it links to the Last Supper on pages 100–101.

- The lamb sacrificed during Passover is unblemished – without a mark and perfect, just as Jesus is completely pure and innocent.
- The lamb was sacrificed to save Jewish people from death, just as Jesus dies to save people from sin and to give them eternal life. John the Baptist called Jesus 'the **Lamb of God**, who takes away the sin of the world' (John 1:29).
- The blood of the lamb was poured out to save the Jewish people, and during the last supper Jesus says 'this is my blood of the covenant, which is poured out for many for the forgiveness of sins' (Matthew 26:28).

▶ *A stained glass image of Jesus as a shepherd, carrying a lost lamb; Jesus is often seen as both a shepherd and a lamb – why do you think this is?*

The Mass as a sacrifice

Although the disciples of Jesus may not have known at the time, Catholics today recognise that Jesus' words during the Last Supper anticipated, and made present in that meal, his sacrificial death on the cross. Jesus spoke of the bread: 'This is my body, which is given for you' (Luke 22:19) and of the wine that is his blood: 'which is poured out for many' (Matthew 26:28). He was pointing toward his future suffering and death. Just as the lamb of the Passover meal was a sacrifice, so Catholics believe Jesus' death on the cross was a sacrifice to free people from the slavery of sin.

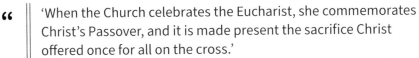

> " 'When the Church celebrates the Eucharist, she commemorates Christ's Passover, and it is made present the sacrifice Christ offered once for all on the cross.'
>
> *Catechism of the Catholic Church 1364*

At the Last Supper, Jesus instituted the Sacrament of the Eucharist as a way to remember and become present at the moment of Jesus' sacrifice on the cross. He told his disciples to share the bread and wine and to 'do this in remembrance of me' (Luke 22:19).

Catholics believe that during Mass Jesus is not just 'represented' in the bread and wine but that 'Christ is mysteriously but really present in the Sacrament of the Eucharist' (YC 216). It is his sacrifice on the cross that makes this possible. Jesus is recognised as the Lamb of God during the Liturgy of the Eucharist in a prayer called the *Agnes Dei*, which is spoken after The Lord's Prayer. Therefore, each time Catholics today celebrate the Eucharist, they not only experience the Real Presence of Jesus, but the events of the Last Supper and the sacrifice Jesus made become really present for them in the Mass.

By regularly celebrating the Mass, Catholics believe that they are honouring Jesus' commandment to 'do this in remembrance of me'. They enter into his sacrifice, drawing closer to God each time they share in the Eucharistic meal with Jesus.

Understand

1 What is the link between Jesus being the Lamb of God and the celebration of Passover?

2 What words does Jesus use about his body and blood at the Last Supper that suggest sacrifice?

3 What does it mean that the Mass is a sacrifice?

4 Explain why Catholics feel it is important to receive the Sacrament of the Eucharist regularly.

Discern

5 'Jesus' sacrifice was the only way for humans to be saved from sin'. Do you agree? Give reasons for your answer.

Respond

6 What sacrifices do you make for others? Do you think that being ready to make serious sacrifices is an important part of being a good person? If so, why?

WHY IS THE STRUCTURE OF THE MASS IMPORTANT?

Catholics have celebrated the Sacrament of the Eucharist since the very beginning of Christianity. The way Mass is celebrated today still reflects traditions and beliefs that can be traced back to the early Church led by St Peter and the apostles. In this lesson you will learn why continuing these traditions through the structure of the Mass remains important to Catholics today.

The ancient tradition of the Mass

The Catholic Church teaches that the way the Mass is celebrated today remains very similar to how Mass was structured at the very beginning of Christianity. The evidence for this can be seen in a letter from St Justin Martyr to the Roman emperor Antoninus Pius, written in AD 155. This letter explained what Christians did during their worship. St Justin Martyr (c. AD 100–165) was an early Christian thinker and saint. Some of his letter to Antoninus Pius is shared in the Catechism (CCC 1345):

> **Link**
>
> Read more about the Liturgy of the Word in the Mass on pages 56–57.

- On Sunday, Christians gathered together in one place for communal worship: 'all who dwell in the city or country gather in the same place'.
- The Mass starts with a reading of the teachings of the apostles, followed by a sermon by the priest who encourages the community to live their life according to those teachings: 'admonishes and challenges them to imitate these beautiful things'.
- The congregation prays together, not just for themselves but 'for all others, wherever they may be', so that God may find them faithful to his laws and they can receive salvation from sin. Those prayers are followed by the sign of peace: 'we exchange the kiss'.
- Priests offer *eucharistian* ('thanksgiving') over the bread and wine, and the congregation prays that they may be worthy of this gift. This is followed by Holy Communion, where the Eucharistic bread and wine are shared among the community and some is saved for 'those who are absent'.

▲ *A thirteenth century painting of The Last Supper from a church in Italy*

It is important to Catholics that the Mass today reflects the way Mass has been celebrated for the last two thousand years, because they believe this shows faithfulness to the teachings of Jesus and the apostles. Sunday Mass today still starts with the Liturgy of the Word, where the scripture and teachings of the apostles are read and a homily is given. It is then followed by the Liturgy of the Eucharist where Christ becomes present when the bread and wine are transformed into his body and blood, which are then shared during Holy Communion. The Church describes this as 'two great parts that … together form "one single act of worship"' (CCC 1346).

The Liturgy of the Eucharist

The Liturgy of the Eucharist is the high point of the Mass. It can be divided into three important parts:

Preparation of the gifts: The Liturgy of the Eucharist begins with members of the congregation taking the bread and wine that will become the body and blood of Jesus to the altar. They also take up the collection of money donated to the Church to support it and to help those who are in need.

Eucharistic prayer: This prayer is the heart of the Liturgy of the Eucharist. During this part, the priest stands in the person of Christ and speaks the words that Jesus spoke during the Last Supper. The sacrifice of Jesus to God the Father is made present to the entire congregation and the bread and wine become the body and blood of Jesus through the process of transubstantiation.

▲ *A stained glass window from a church in Normandy, France; it shows St Joan of Arc with soldiers from the First World War taking part in the Sacrament of Eucharist*

Communion rite: The last part of the Liturgy of the Eucharist unites the congregation as a community. It begins with everyone praying The Lord's Prayer together and then sharing a sign of peace in the form of a bow or a handshake with their neighbour. The priest breaks the bread, just as Jesus did at the Last Supper and at the supper at Emmaus, then the congregation sing together an *Agnus Dei* prayer – a reminder that Jesus is the Lamb of God. Finally, people receive the body and blood of Jesus in Holy Communion.

Link

Read more about Jesus as the Lamb of God on pages 108–109.

Understand

1 Who was St Justin Martyr?
2 Name three things that were part of communal worship for the early Christians.
3 Give two similarities and one difference between the Mass today and the practices of the early Christians.
4 What are the three main parts of the Liturgy of the Eucharist?

Discern

5 'The Eucharistic prayer is the most important part of the Mass.' How might a Catholic respond to this statement?
6 Do you think that following ancient traditions has a place in twenty-first century religious worship?

Respond

7 Can you think of any traditions that remain important to you and your family over many years. How important is tradition to you?

HOW DO CATHOLICS CARRY JESUS INTO THE WORLD?

OBJECTIVES

In this lesson you will consider **how the Eucharist strengthens Catholics in their Christian mission in the world.**

As we have read, the word 'Mass' comes from *missio*, the Latin term for 'mission', meaning a duty or a calling. The Church teaches that when Catholics receive the body and blood of Jesus, they also receive a mission to share the love of God with the world. The body and the blood also give them the strength to carry out this mission faithfully.

The Church as a community

We have seen how receiving the Eucharist unites Catholics together as one Church community. In the Bible, there are many descriptions of the early Church community, including the way they worshipped as a group. In **Acts of the Apostles**, we can read that the first Christians 'devoted themselves to the apostles' teaching and the fellowship, to the breaking of bread and the prayers' (Acts: 2:42). Furthermore, the Christian community was committed to acts of love and charity, with its members selling all their possessions to help people in poverty.

▲ *Food bank staff and volunteers at St Margaret's Church in South London packing food parcels to support people in need*

From this we know then that, from the very beginning, Christians were united by:
- the teachings of the apostles
- the Sacrament of the Eucharist
- shared prayers
- acts of charity and love.

The Church teaches that the Catholic community today is united in exactly the same way. The Catechism explains that the Eucharist commits Catholics to serve the poor because Jesus taught that he was present in every person in need. If you receive the body and blood of Jesus, you therefore have to recognise the presence of Jesus in all those who are in poverty or in need. Your mission is then the same as his: to show mercy and love through your actions and to share God's message.

After Catholics receive Jesus in the Eucharist, each Mass ends with particular words of dismissal. These command the congregation to go out into the world and carry Jesus with them to show love and kindness to those in need. The dismissal can be expressed in four different ways:

‘Go forth, the Mass is ended.’   ‘Go and announce the Gospel of the Lord.’

‘Go in peace.’   ‘Go in peace, glorifying the Lord by your life.’

> **Useful vocabulary**
>
> **Acts of the Apostles:** a book in the New Testament which describes the beginning of the early Church, similar in style to a Gospel

Is serving those in need more important than the Eucharist?

Serving those who live in poverty or are in need has always been an important part of Catholic mission. Does this mean that this is a more important part of being a Catholic than celebrating the Eucharist? Think about these different arguments:

Serving those in poverty is more important	Celebrating the Eucharist is more important
Showing love and kindness to others and working selflessly as stewards of creation have practical benefits to the wider world. These are things that can be seen and felt and are more important than simply remembering the Last Supper.	Celebration of the Eucharist is more than simply remembering the Last Supper. In the Eucharist, Catholics can experience the Real Presence of Jesus and be united with God as a community. This union with God is the ultimate purpose of human life.
In the Gospels, Jesus constantly teaches the importance of serving those in poverty. Serving all those in need is more important than celebration of the Eucharist because it is a way to live one's life following Jesus' example.	In all the Gospels, Jesus commands his disciples to celebrate the Eucharist when he says 'Do this in remembrance of me' (Luke 22:19). By receiving the body of Jesus, Catholics not only follow Jesus' teachings, but become part of the Body of the Church and receive grace, essential for living a full, faithful life.
Acts of the Apostles describes how, from the very beginning, Christians sold all their possessions to give to those who were in need. Christians shared all they had and lived a simple life dedicated to showing love and kindness. Serving those in poverty was the most essential part of their mission.	In Acts of the Apostles, the sharing of bread, which is the Sacrament of the Eucharist, is repeated numerous times as the most essential practice of the early Church. The story of the Road to Emmaus (Luke 24:13–35) teaches that it is in the breaking of the bread that Christians are able to know God.

Individual Catholics may feel both are equally important, but the Catholic Church teaches that the Sacrament of the Eucharist is the '**source and summit**' of Christian life and all the good works they do as Catholics are '**bound up with the Eucharist and are oriented toward it**' (CCC 1324). This suggests that while helping the poor is essential, it is the Eucharist that gives Catholics the grace necessary to show true love and kindness to those who are in need, and the strength to face obstacles that could get in the way of helping others.

Link

Read more about the responsibility of Catholics to help others on pages 24–25.

Understand

1 What is the meaning of the word 'Mass'?

2 What practices united the early Church together?

3 What does the Eucharist teach Catholics, concerning those who live in poverty?

4 How does the Mass encourage Catholics to act at the end of the service?

Discern

5 Read through the reasons in favour of the view that serving the poor is more important than celebrating the Eucharist. Which of those reasons do you find most persuasive and why?

6 'It is more important to serve the poor than to celebrate the Eucharist.' Do you agree? How might a Catholic respond to this statement?

Respond

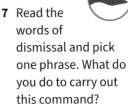

7 Read the words of dismissal and pick one phrase. What do you do to carry out this command?

WHAT DO DIFFERENT CHRISTIANS BELIEVE ABOUT THE EUCHARIST?

The Catholic Church believes that the celebration of the Eucharist is special because it contains 'the whole spiritual good of the Church, namely Christ himself' (CCC 1324). When other Christian **denominations** celebrate the Eucharist, they too honour the sacrifice Jesus made on the cross, but they may celebrate and think about how Jesus is present in a very different way, showing there is a rich diversity in Christian belief and practice.

What do Protestants believe about the Real Presence?

There are many different Protestant denominations, or Churches, including Anglican, Presbyterian, Methodist and Baptist, to name just a few. There are also different traditions within these Churches, for example: Anglicans may be Anglo-Catholic, Liberal or Evangelical. Among these different denominations, there is a variety of beliefs regarding the celebration of the Last Supper, for example, most Protestants would reject the Catholic belief that the Eucharist *makes present* the sacrifice of Jesus. They may hold different beliefs on the Real Presence of Jesus.

- Protestants offer a variety of explanations as to *how* Jesus is really present in the bread and wine. Most Anglicans believe that Jesus is really *spiritually* present, through **consubstantiation**, which means that the bread and wine are both the body and blood of Jesus *and* bread and wine at the same time.
- Some Protestants believe that Jesus' Real Presence can only be received during Holy Communion if a person accepts the sacrament with faith and is worthy of receiving it. This view is known as receptionism.
- Some Protestants, for example Baptists, believe that the Eucharist, which they usually call the Lord's Supper, commemorates the Last Supper. They believe it is a way to re-enact the events of the Last Supper, and that the bread and wine are simply symbols of Jesus' death and resurrection.

> **Useful vocabulary**
>
> **denominations:** branches of the Christian Church

▲ *A celebration of the Eucharist in an Anglican church*

What do Eastern Orthodox Churches believe about the Real Presence?

The **Eastern Orthodox** Church accepts both the belief in the Real Presence of Jesus in the Eucharist, and the belief that Jesus' sacrifice is made present to those who receive the sacrament. Orthodox Christians believe that the Real Presence of Jesus is a mystery – which means that they do not try to explain how Jesus is present in the bread and wine.

How do different Churches celebrate the Eucharist?

In the Catholic Church, celebrations of the Eucharist can happen daily and Catholics are expected to attend Mass every Sunday. Orthodox Christians share the Catholic view that celebrating the Eucharist is a central part of Christian worship. Like Catholics, they celebrate the sacrament every Sunday, reflecting its importance within their faith. Protestant Churches usually celebrate the Eucharist once a week. This day may vary between denominations to be Sunday (for example, Anglicans) or Saturday. In other congregations, the Sacrament of the Eucharist is celebrated only occasionally and can take second place to the Liturgy of the Word. Some Christians, such as Quakers, do not celebrate the Eucharist.

Anglicans only recognise two sacraments: the Eucharist and Baptism. In the Church of England, the central part of the Sacrament of the Eucharist is the prayer of thanksgiving.

The special attention Christians give to both the presentation and storing of the Eucharist reflects their belief in the Real Presence. Those Christians that believe that Jesus is present in the sacrament want to show their reverence by using special items that draw attention to the sacrament. Nearly all Churches that celebrate the Eucharist use a chalice (cup) to hold the wine and a paten or diskos (plate) for the bread. Catholic and Eastern Orthodox churches also have a tabernacle (holy cupboard) to store the consecrated host saved after the Eucharist. The tabernacle was first introduced to reserve the Blessed Sacrament in a worthy place so that it could be taken to the sick who were unable to attend Mass. Over the centuries, it has become a very important sign of the Real Presence of Christ with his people in the Blessed Sacrament and is the focus of silent adoration and private prayer. Catholics will always genuflect to the tabernacle (bending one knee to touch the floor) when they enter and leave a church.

▲ A golden tabernacle to store the consecrated host

Understand

1 Give two different beliefs about the Real Presence of Jesus in the Eucharist or Lord's Supper.

2 What do most Anglicans believe about the Eucharist?

3 What is a tabernacle? Explain its purpose in a Catholic Church.

Discern

4 To what extent do the different Christian celebrations reflect different Christian beliefs about the Eucharist?

Respond

5 Many Christians have very different views of the Eucharist. Does this make you think differently about your own views?

Link 🔗

To learn about some ways in which the Blessed Sacrament is honoured by Catholics, read pages 120–121 about processions of the Blessed Sacrament.

HOW CAN WE RESPOND TO WORLD HUNGER?

Eating together is one of the most common themes of the Gospels. Jesus taught his followers to feed the hungry, and in the Eucharistic prayer, Catholics thank God for the gifts of food and drink which bring them together with God as a Christian family. The current world food crisis therefore means that Catholics don't just feel an ethical duty to help those in need, they feel a religious duty too.

The world food crisis: an ethical issue

In 1990 the United Nations estimated there to be one billion people in the world who faced hunger or starvation. Even though the population of the world grew, this figure steadily reduced over the years. However, the World Food Organisation reported that since 2019, the number of people who face genuine risk of hunger has started to go up again. There are several different reasons for this, including:

- more conflicts around the world, making it dangerous or difficult to farm land
- climate change causing problems for farmers such as droughts and floods, leaving less food to be harvested
- economic consequences from conflicts and events such as global pandemics, making food too expensive for many people to buy.

▲ *A farmer walks through rice paddy fields in Thailand; the fields are dry due to very hot weather and drought, a result of climate change*

This is known as 'food insecurity' and millions around the world face the possibility of starvation. Catholics, like all people, are faced with the ethical question of how they should help those struggling in the world food crisis.

How Catholic teachings about the Eucharist link to the food crisis

Food plays an important role in the Bible. In the creation story, no other necessity of life is mentioned apart from food. As we have read, the most important part of the celebration of the Passover was a shared meal. In the Mass, Catholics can experience Christ's presence through his Word and through the community of the Church, but his Real Presence comes through the bread and wine which become his body and blood in the shared meal of the Eucharist. The Church teaches that one of the reasons why the Eucharist is so important is because it connects those who receive it:

> " 'Because there is one bread, we who are many are one body, for we all partake of the one bread.'
>
> *Catechism of the Catholic Church 1396*

Who is Bishop Theotonius Gomes?

One Catholic leader who has raised awareness of food insecurity is Bishop Theotonius Gomes from Bangladesh. He teaches Catholics that the Sacrament of the Eucharist should remind them that human beings are a balance of physical body and spiritual soul. Both of these are essential for living a whole and full life, and both need to be cared for.

▲ *Bishop Theotonius Gomes*

> " 'Lack of food for the poor, especially large numbers dying of hunger, is the most "un-eucharistic" situation on earth. This is a darkness on human civilisation in our advanced times.'
>
> *Bishop Theotonius Gomes 'World Food Day Reflection from Bangladesh'*

Bishop Gomes suggests that in today's world, where so many people have plentiful food and water, the current food crisis is unnecessary and a problem that should be solved. He suggests that, if we think of ourselves as really civilised human beings who treat one another with respect and dignity, then we must meet every person's basic needs. Allowing others to go hungry is the 'darkness' which suggests we may not be as civilised as we think we are. Bishop Gomes calls all Catholics to work against this darkness. Breaking bread with others is one of the essential parts of Catholic life, so Bishop Gomes believes acting to solve the food crisis is not just the right thing to do, it is deeply linked with Catholic beliefs about the Eucharist.

What can Catholics do to help?

CAFOD is a charity that tackles the consequences of the global food crisis in the UK. It is also part of an international network of Catholic organisations called Caritas who are working to help people affected by the food crisis around the world. CAFOD raises awareness about the current food crisis, as well as working with local communities to provide food, water and other practical help to those in need.

Individual Catholics, even those who are still young, are encouraged to do the following to help with the mounting food crisis:

- Support organisations that help those who are most vulnerable. Catholics can donate food or volunteer to help people in the UK, or support CAFOD's work by donating money or fundraising to help communities overseas.
- Take part in campaigns that urge the government to do more to help those affected by the food crisis. Making your voice heard is one of the best ways to make change happen.
- Pray for those affected by hunger and food insecurity. When Catholics pray The Lord's Prayer: 'Give us our daily bread', they can think of those around the world who are most in need of food.

Discern

4 Which cause of food insecurity do you think is most significant? Why?

5 Do you agree with Bishop Gomes that world hunger is a 'darkness on human civilisation'? Give reasons for your answer.

Respond

6 Research what other Catholics have said about the world food crisis. What positive ideas can you take from them to make a difference in your community?

Understand

1 Give three reasons for food insecurity in the world.
2 What does Bishop Gomes call all Catholics to do?
3 Name two things that Catholics can do to help deal with the world food crisis.

WHAT CAN ART TEACH US ABOUT THE EUCHARIST?

OBJECTIVES

In this lesson you will explore different artistic expressions of the Last Supper and the Eucharist.

From the very beginning of the Church, art was used to teach key events from the life of Jesus and to explore the important ideas of Christian faith. It is not surprising then that the Last Supper and the Sacrament of the Eucharist have been two of the most popular topics for artists over the centuries. Here are two artworks that explore these topics.

The *Life of Jesus Mafa: The Last Supper*

This representation of the Last Supper is part of a series of paintings created in the 1970s in Cameroon known as the *Life of Jesus Mafa*. The Mafa people are indigenous to Cameroon (meaning they were among the first people to have lived there). This project was a collaboration between Catholic priests, thinkers and community leaders to make the stories of the Gospel more real and relevant to people in Cameroon. It shows Jesus and his disciples as African men, living and teaching in everyday environments that would be familiar to Cameroonians.

The painting explores two central themes of the Eucharist:

Link

Read more about the *Life of Jesus Mafa* series on page 146.

The communion of the Church: This is shown in the presentation of the disciples as members of the local African community; the use of a bowl to drink from, linking to the dishes and customs of local community life; the presence of familiar items around the table, such as a drum and water-pitcher, to show that everybody is invited to join the community of the Church, united around the Sacrament of the Eucharist.

The Real Presence of Christ in the sacrament: This is suggested by the striking red cloak worn by Jesus; the use of light to draw attention to him and mark him out from his disciples; the glowing golden bowl to suggest riches and to remind viewers of God's glory.

Last Supper by Pascal Dagnan-Bouveret

This version of the Last Supper was created in 1896 by a French painter, Pascal Dagnan-Bouveret. This painting of the Last Supper is a very traditional representation of the events of the institution of the Eucharist. Jesus is placed at the centre of the painting, surrounded by mysterious light and holding a cup of wine; Jesus' disciples sitting on either side are watching the sacrament intently and in wonder. The heavenly light subtly hints at the miraculous nature of the event and the importance of Jesus' presence at the centre of it all.

Understand

1 Why is the Last Supper a popular topic in Catholic art?

2 What was the purpose behind the creation of the series of paintings called the *Life of Jesus Mafa*?

3 Give two ways *Life of Jesus Mafa: The Last Supper* shows the significance of the Eucharist.

Discern

4 Look at the *Life of Jesus Mafa: The Last Supper*. What ideas about the Eucharist do you think the artist was trying to show? Compare and contrast this painting with Pascal Dagnan-Bouveret's *Last Supper*.

5 Which of these two artworks do you think best represents Catholic beliefs about the Eucharist? Explain your answer.

Respond

6 Do these paintings reflect what you have learned about the Eucharist or make you think about it in a different way?

OBJECTIVES

In this lesson you will learn **how the Real Presence of Jesus is honoured in the processions of the Blessed Sacrament.**

HOW DO PROCESSIONS OF THE BLESSED SACRAMENT HONOUR JESUS?

Catholics around the world show their faith in the Real Presence of Jesus in the Sacrament of the Eucharist in a variety of ways. Catholics believe that Jesus remains present in the consecrated **host**, or Blessed Sacrament, forever. As you have learned, some of the Blessed Sacrament is always kept after Mass. One of the most spectacular forms of devotion in Catholic tradition is the procession of the Blessed Sacrament.

The Blessed Sacrament

Catholics believe that during the Sacrament of the Eucharist, the bread and wine become the real body and blood of Jesus Christ in a process called transubstantiation. From that moment, the consecrated host is also known as the Blessed Sacrament. As it is believed to be the Real Presence of Jesus, it is treated with awe and devotion.

What are the processions of the Blessed Sacrament?

One of the oldest ways for Catholics around the world to worship or honour the Blessed Sacrament are Eucharistic processions. During these processions, the Blessed Sacrament is displayed in a monstrance – a decorative frame – and carried publicly around a holy site. Sometimes these occasions are solemn, sometimes they are more joyous – this may depend on the country in which they take place. Some processions are small and might involve carrying the Blessed Sacrament around the inside of the church, but some are huge events where the Blessed Sacrament is carried from one holy site to another through a crowded city. As Catholics believe Jesus is present in the Blessed Sacrament, they also believe that he walks with them during the procession.

The Feast of **Corpus Christi** takes place on the second Thursday after Pentecost Sunday. On this important Catholic feast day, a procession is a way to proclaim to the world the Catholic belief in the Real Presence of Jesus in the Eucharist, and to share him with those who join in or watch. It is a celebration, but also a solemn and dignified event.

> **Useful vocabulary**
>
> **host:** the holy bread of the Eucharist
>
> **Corpus Christi:** the Latin phrase for 'body of Christ'; a feast that celebrates the Real Presence of Christ in the Blessed Sacrament

► *Celebrations of Corpus Christi in Poland*

Tradition and culture in processions

Processions of the Blessed Sacrament are occasions for Catholics around the world to incorporate their own culture and traditions into their devotion to Jesus. In Poland, large crowds of people wear traditional dress and elaborate decorations, then come together to walk through villages, towns or cities. In Brazil, streets are decorated with bright colours, people wear colourful costumes and rhythmic drums are played as the procession moves along. There may be a 'tapete', a carpet of dyed sawdust laid out in religious patterns for the procession to walk over.

▲ *Streets in Brazil are decorated in bright colours for the celebration of Corpus Christi*

Processions of the Blessed Sacrament are often full of beauty and cultural variety. Traditions from different countries, such as the Brazilian tapete, are now used in processions in other countries. Banners and other decorations may also be used but the display of the Blessed Sacrament is the most important part of the procession.

Catholic teaching on processions of the Blessed Sacrament

The Catholic Church teaches that processions of the Blessed Sacrament are a faithful form of worship. The Church provides advice on how to include cultural elements thoughtfully so they do not distract from the purpose of the procession – the veneration of the Blessed Sacrament. The Church believes processions are a way to publicly celebrate faith and belonging to the Church community, as well as a way to bring the presence of Jesus to everyone in a highly visual celebration.

Understand

1 What do Catholics mean by the term 'Blessed Sacrament'?

2 Why do Catholics treat the Blessed Sacrament with awe and devotion?

3 What are processions of the Blessed Sacrament?

4 What do Catholics celebrate during the feast of Corpus Christi?

5 Give two examples of how Catholic communities around the world show their culture and traditions in these processions.

Discern

6 Processions of the Blessed Sacrament can express Catholic beliefs about the Eucharist as well as the culture and traditions of a particular group of people. Which do you think is more important, expressing beliefs, culture or both? Explain your view.

Respond

7 Do you find the different processions of the Blessed Sacrament inspiring? Why or why not?

ASSESSMENT

Key vocabulary

Write a definition for these key terms.

Paschal Mystery	**sacrament**	**Passover**	**Eucharist**
Sacrifice of the Mass	**transubstantiation**	**Holy Communion**	**Lord's Supper**
Blessed Sacrament			

Knowledge check

1 Which of the following is another name for the Sacrament of the Eucharist?

   a Last Supper

   b Holy Communion

   c Blessed Meal

2 Copy out and complete the following sentence:

   Catholics believe that the b................. and b................. of Jesus are a sacrifice that provides salvation to all humans.

3 Name one of the Sacraments of Initiation.

4 What is Passover?

5 Explain what sacraments are.

6 What are the two most important parts of the Mass?

7 Give two ways in which Jesus is present during the celebration of the Mass.

8 How do the words and actions of Jesus connect the Old Testament and the New Testament?

9 Explain two different views about the Eucharist among Christians today.

10 In what ways is Mass today similar to the way Mass was celebrated among early Christians?

TIP

Before you start writing, think about different Christian denominations and how they celebrate the Eucharist. You might find it useful to discuss how the different ways they celebrate show their beliefs.

Extended writing activity

This assessment is for you to show what you have learned in this chapter and to develop your extended writing skills. Here is a big question:

Explain why many Catholics believe the Eucharist is the most important practice. Why do some Christians have other views?

This can be broken down into two smaller questions. Your teacher will direct you to which questions they want you to answer.

TIP

Explain how the celebration of the Eucharist is important for Christians. In this chapter we explored several different reasons why this sacrament is significant for Catholics (for example, see pages 102–103), as well as how other Christian denominations celebrate the Eucharist (see pages 114–115). Use some of this information to help you write your answer.

1 **Why do many Catholics consider the Eucharist to be the most important Christian practice?**

You could use 'Point-Evidence-Explain' to write at least one paragraph to answer this question.

Point – make the point for your paragraph

Evidence – give evidence to back up your point

Explain – what the evidence means and how it answers the question

Here is an example:

The Catholic Church teaches that Christians can experience the Real o⋯⋯⋯ Presence of Jesus in the Sacrament of the Eucharist. During the Liturgy of the Eucharist, the priest speaks the same words that Jesus spoke o⋯⋯⋯ during the Last Supper: 'This is my body… this is my blood'. Through these words the bread and wine really become the body and blood of Jesus in the process known as transubstantiation. Catholics believe that by receiving this body and blood, they form a union with God. This clearly shows the o⋯⋯⋯ significance of the Sacrament of the Eucharist as the most important practice to help Catholics get closer to God.

1 A **point** is made in this first sentence.

2 There is **evidence** to back up the point in the second and third sentences.

3 This sentence **explains** what the evidence means and how it answers the question.

Words you could use:

sacrifice   Blessed Sacrament   Holy Communion   transubstantiation
Mass   Real Presence   'source and summit'

2 **Explain why other Christians might not agree that the Eucharist is the most important practice.**

Write at least one paragraph explaining how other Christians view the Eucharist. You might find these sentence starters helpful.

Not all Christians view the Eucharist in the same way. For example…

Eastern Orthodox Christians believe…

Some Protestants believe…

Words you could use:

consubstantiation   re-enact
Quakers   Anglicans

TIP

Explain one or two beliefs of other Christian denominations about the Eucharist.

Try to write at least one more paragraph explaining what other Christian practices might be seen as more important than the Eucharist.

Ideas you could use:

prayer   serving those in need

TIP

What might some Christians believe is more important than the Eucharist? You could re-read page 113 for some ideas.

TO THE ENDS OF THE EARTH

Introduction

When Jesus had ascended into heaven, people could have been mistaken in thinking that his work was done. However, **Christians believe that before Jesus ascended, he told his apostles what he needed them to do to continue his work: they were to go out into the world and build up a community of believers**. 'To the ends of the earth' means that Jesus' message needed to be spread to all people, in all places and for all time.

Jesus knew that his apostles would find this difficult. The message they were going to preach would be different to anything that people had heard before and they would face lots of challenges fulfilling their mission, so **Jesus promised that he would send them the Holy Spirit**. Catholics believe that the Holy Spirit is the third person of the Trinity and, so, is God.

Catholics believe that the Holy Spirit guided the apostles to help them to bring about the Church community on earth. They believe that **the same Holy Spirit guides individual people and the whole Church community on earth still today.**

Catholics, and many other Christians, see the Holy Spirit as a really important reminder of God's love for humans. The role of the Holy Spirit is particularly prominent in St Luke's Gospel and Acts of the Apostles – St Luke mentions the Holy Spirit in these texts more than in the other three Gospels combined. **The Holy Spirit means that humans can never feel alone or that they can't do something**; the Holy Spirit gives gifts to encourage and help people to do even those things they think are beyond their reach. This means that Christians ask the Holy Spirit to help them – either through receiving the Holy Spirit in the Sacrament of Confirmation, or on a daily basis through prayer.

Catholics believe that the Holy Spirit's power can be seen in how a person lives: if they are filled with the Spirit, they show this in their attitudes and behaviour.

Pentecost is so important that it is celebrated every year. Some countries have unique traditions to show the importance of the festival. Many individuals have explored what Pentecost means to them through art, linking their cultural experience with their religious beliefs to show how **the story of Pentecost is both life-changing and exciting and remains important for Christians today**.

OBJECTIVES

In this lesson you will learn about **the author of two New Testament books: Luke's Gospel and the Acts of the Apostles.**

WHO WAS ST LUKE?

St Luke is believed to have written both Luke's Gospel and the Acts of the Apostles. Luke's Gospel tells us about the life, death and resurrection of Jesus. Acts of the Apostles tells us about the time that the apostles and Mary, Jesus' mother, received the Holy Spirit, as well as how the early Church grew.

St Luke the author

Catholics believe that the Bible is the inspired word of God. God guided humans, through the Holy Spirit, to write down God's word. One such person was St Luke, who is described as an **evangelist**. To evangelise is to spread the Good News about Jesus, and Luke did this through his Gospel.

Luke's Gospel is one of four Gospels found in the New Testament. It was probably written around AD 85–90. Luke doesn't name himself directly as the author of the Gospel, however he tells his readers that he didn't ever directly meet Jesus himself. He explains at the start of his Gospel that he was writing an account using the evidence of 'eye-witnesses and ministers of the word' that had been passed to him (Luke 1:2).

▲ *A stained glass image showing St Luke the Evangelist*

Luke was a companion of St Paul, which is mentioned in Acts and in some of St Paul's letters. In St Paul's letter to the Colossians, he refers to Luke as his 'beloved physician' (Colossians 4:14). A physician is a doctor, which helps us to understand that Luke was an intelligent and well-educated man.

Luke's Gospel ends with Jesus ascending into heaven but, unlike the other Gospels, Luke continues into a second book – the Acts of the Apostles. Acts picks up from the Ascension and tells, in lots of detail, how the early Christian community continued after Jesus had gone to God in heaven. He gives details about how the community organised itself, worshiped and told the Good News about Jesus to other people.

Why do people believe Luke wrote both books?

At the beginning of Luke's Gospel, he addresses his writings to 'Theophilus', which means 'Lover of God', as an 'orderly account' of everything that he had come to believe (Luke 1:1–4). At the beginning of Acts, Luke writes 'In the first book, O Theophilus…' (Acts 1:1) and explains that the Gospel had been about Jesus' life and that he had told the apostles to remain in Jerusalem to wait for the Holy Spirit. Following this, Luke writes about the Ascension and what happened following this event.

Useful vocabulary

evangelist: someone who spreads the Good News about Jesus; also the title used to refer to the four Gospel writers: Matthew, Mark, Luke and John

What did St Luke want to communicate?

In his Gospel, Luke places a special emphasis on people who were often left out of society. In Jesus' time, lots of people were treated as second-class citizens, such as people who were sick, disabled or had broken the law. Luke shows how much Jesus loved all people, but that the people who were left out of society were shown particular care.

Luke also gives prominence to women in his Gospel. For example, he writes about Anna, a prophetess who blesses Jesus (Luke 2:36–38) and in Luke's Gospel the angel Gabriel tells Mary that she will bear the Son of God (Luke 1:26–38) – in Matthew's Gospel the angel makes the annunciation to Joseph, not Mary. Luke is making it clear that Jesus' forgiveness and salvation was for all people.

In Luke's Gospel and Acts, the Holy Spirit is given a prominent role. The Holy Spirit is mentioned 58 times over both books, and only 14 times in the other three Gospels. In Luke's Gospel, Jesus describes himself as anointed by the Holy Spirit to do this work, when he reads from the prophet Isaiah in the synagogue (Luke 4:18–19). Isaiah describes his work as helping people who were poor, oppressed, in captivity and blind; just the kinds of people who suffered in society at the time of Jesus.

▲ *Jesus healing the sick*

Luke finishes his Gospel with the promise of the Holy Spirit. In Acts, he tells the story of the apostles receiving the Holy Spirit at Pentecost (Acts 2:1–12) and how the Holy Spirit guides the Church community and helps it to grow and bring the Good News about Jesus to even more people. Just as in his Gospel, Luke makes it clear that anyone can become a Christian and Acts contains lots of evidence of people converting to Christianity. This includes Saul, who had persecuted Christians but later became a Christian and went on to help establish the Church as St Paul.

Link

Read more about Jesus' reading in the synagogue on pages 132–133.

Understand

1 How did St Luke evangelise?
2 What did Luke say he relied on to write his Gospel?
3 What did Luke place a special emphasis on in his Gospel?
4 What evidence is there to show that Luke wrote both the Gospel of Luke and Acts?
5 Who did Luke believe Jesus' forgiveness and salvation were for?
6 How did Luke show the importance of the Holy Spirit in this Gospel and the Acts of the Apostles?

Discern

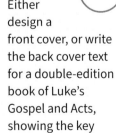

7 'St Luke's emphasis on those left out of society is an important message for Christians today.' Do you agree with this? Give reasons for your answer.

Respond

8 Either design a front cover, or write the back cover text for a double-edition book of Luke's Gospel and Acts, showing the key messages of both.

WHO IS THE HOLY SPIRIT?

OBJECTIVES

In this lesson you will learn about **the Holy Spirit and the symbols used to represent it.**

Christians believe that there is one God, who is three persons: the Father, the Son and the **Holy Spirit**. Each person of the Trinity is God and so the Holy Spirit, the third person of the Trinity, is fully and truly God. The Holy Spirit plays an important role in the life of the Church and in guiding and helping individual Christians in their lives.

The Holy Spirit

Christians believe that God's power is seen all around us. The Holy Spirit is the power of God at work in the world every day, helping people to know God and to allow God to guide them in their lives. The Bible uses imagery to communicate about the work of the Holy Spirit and to help humans to understand the ways in which the Holy Spirit can work in their lives. This helps Catholics to have faith and follow Jesus.

The symbols of the Holy Spirit

Symbols are used to help humans to understand ideas about God that they might find difficult to grasp. There are lots of different symbols of the Holy Spirit that Catholics use to explore and understand the Holy Spirit.

Water

Water is used to show that, at Baptism, a person is washed clean of sin and given new life through the Holy Spirit. Their new life is as a follower of Jesus and the new life comes from Jesus' love, which was shown most clearly when he was crucified. Their new life is a sharing in the eternal life Jesus made possible through his death on the cross.

Anointing and the seal

In the Old Testament, people who were given a special role by God were anointed with oil (this means they had oil put on their bodies in a special ceremony that set them apart to carry out their special task). In the Sacrament of **Confirmation**, the candidate is anointed with oil to show how they are called by the Holy Spirit to serve God in their lives. The Holy Spirit helped people to understand that Jesus was the anointed one (this is what the titles 'Messiah' and 'Christ' mean) and also helps Christians today to live for God. In Baptism, Confirmation and Holy Orders (when a man takes vows to become a priest), a candidate is 'sealed' with the Holy Spirit, showing that a person has been forever changed by the Holy Spirit, just like when a seal is pressed into wax and leaves an impression.

Useful vocabulary

Holy Spirit: the third person of the Trinity, true God, who Christians believe inspires people

Confirmation: the Sacrament of Initiation that completes Baptism and strengthens a person's faith by being sealed with the Holy Spirit as a mature member of the Church

Pentecost: a Christian festival celebrating the time when the Holy Spirit came down to the apostles; also a Jewish festival known as Shavuot, celebrating the harvest and the giving of the Torah at Mount Sinai

Fire and wind

Both fire and wind have great power and energy. They can change things. Christians also believe that the Holy Spirit has these qualities. In the Bible, when the disciples receive the Holy Spirit at **Pentecost**, it appears as flames that touch the disciples on their heads. They are changed from being scared to having courage and are filled with the power and energy to spread the Good News about Jesus.

Cloud and light

When Moses encountered God on Mount Sinai, he appears as cloud and light. And when Jesus is transfigured before his disciples, he glows like light and the voice of God speaks from the cloud. The cloud and light are symbols of the Holy Spirit, revealing God's glory (the light) and God's transcendence (the cloud).

The hand

When Jesus healed and blessed people, he laid his hands on them. He instructed the apostles to lay their hands on others in blessing and so, even today, the laying of hands is used to show the Holy Spirit's power being given to someone, for example in the Sacrament of Confirmation.

The finger

In Luke's Gospel, Jesus speaks about driving out demons by the finger of God and, in Exodus, God is described as writing the Ten Commandments using a finger. St Paul says in his letter to the Hebrews that Jesus writes God's law onto people's hearts with his finger. This shows that the Holy Spirit has the power to change people.

The dove

This is a very traditional image for the Holy Spirit. In the Bible story, when the earth is safe again after the flood, a dove returns to Noah with an olive branch and when Jesus was baptised, a dove came from the heavens. The dove is a symbol of God's power to purify.

Understand

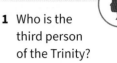

1 Who is the third person of the Trinity?

2 What important role does the Holy Spirit have in the life of the Church and of individuals?

3 Why are symbols used to show the Holy Spirit?

4 Give two reasons why fire is used as a symbol of the Holy Spirit.

5 What was happening to Jesus when the Holy Spirit appeared as a dove?

Discern

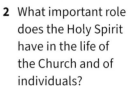

6 Choose the three most appropriate adjectives to describe the Holy Spirit from this list: powerful, cleansing, life-changing, energising, terrifying, kind, judgemental, all-knowing. Explain why you think these adjectives best describe the Holy Spirit.

Respond

7 Do you pray? If so, how far would you say that your prayers are led by the Holy Spirit?

OBJECTIVES

In this lesson you will explore **the important role that the Holy Spirit played in Jesus' life.**

WHAT ROLE DID THE HOLY SPIRIT PLAY IN JESUS' LIFE?

Jesus' time on earth showed God's power and love to humans. God's power and love meant that the impossible was possible through Jesus, helping people to see that Jesus was the incarnate Son of God, which gave them the faith and courage to follow Jesus. If we explore stories about Jesus, from before he was born to when he rose to heaven, we see that the Holy Spirit is present at important moments in Jesus' life.

The Holy Spirit is present at key moments in Jesus' life

In Luke's Gospel, we read the story of the angel Gabriel appearing to Mary and telling her that she will give birth to the Son of God. There's an important detail in this story – Mary won't conceive Jesus like other humans are conceived; the Holy Spirit will miraculously make Mary pregnant without any human father. When the angel tells Mary that her relative Elizabeth (who was very old and couldn't have children) is also pregnant, he reminds Mary:

> " 'For nothing will be impossible with God.'
>
> *Luke 1:37*

The Holy Spirit show's God's great power to make the impossible, possible.

As an adult, Jesus was baptised by Elizabeth's son John the Baptist. John had been baptising people as a symbol of repentance or wanting to turn away from sin. However, Jesus' baptism by John was different. He didn't need to repent. In Luke's Gospel it says that when Jesus had been baptised:

> " 'the heavens were opened, and the Holy Spirit descended on him in bodily form, like a dove; and a voice came from heaven, "You are my beloved Son; with you I am well pleased."'
>
> *Luke 3:21–22*

▼ *The Annunciation is the story of the angel Gabriel appearing to Mary and telling her that she will give birth to the Son of God*

This moment shows that God the Father (the voice from the heavens), the Son (Jesus) and the Holy Spirit (the dove) are all different persons but also one God. God's voice tells us that Jesus is God's son and the Holy Spirit shows how God brings peace and purity, and helps people to have a new start. This is why Christians today are baptised.

The Holy Spirit guided Jesus to do God's work

Shortly after being baptised, the Holy Spirit guides Jesus back to Galilee and he goes to the synagogue in Nazareth, the town he grew up in. He reads from the Torah Scrolls, speaking words from the prophet Isaiah, who lived about 700 years before Jesus but wrote about the Messiah. Jesus reads:

> 'The Spirit of the Lord is upon me, because he has anointed me'
>
> *Luke 4:18*

This means that God's Spirit is with Jesus because he will do God's work to:
- proclaim Good News to the poor
- free captives and people who are oppressed
- help blind people see.

These are all ways of describing how Jesus will help people who can use God's love and power to have a new life in Jesus. It didn't just mean that Jesus would heal people who were literally blind, but he would also help those who couldn't see the truth because they didn't have faith. He is telling the world that he is building God's Kingdom on earth and that the Holy Spirit is helping this to happen.

The Holy Spirit helps others to do God's work

Jesus' death showed God's power too, since Catholics believe that three days after he died on the cross the Holy Spirit raised Jesus from the dead. No ordinary human can do this, but Christians believe that Jesus did rise from the dead because he was the Son of God and because the Holy Spirit made this possible. At the end of Luke's Gospel, before Jesus rises into heaven, he tells his disciples that he is:

> 'sending the promise of my Father upon you.'
>
> *Luke 24:49*

This promise was the Holy Spirit and would help them to carry on Jesus' work on earth.

Understand

1 What does Luke 1 tell us about how Jesus was conceived?
2 What happened just after Jesus was baptised?
3 What did Jesus tell people he was anointed by the Holy Spirit to do?
4 What do Christians believe happened three days after Jesus' death?
5 What did Jesus promise to his disciples before he ascended into heaven?

Discern

6 'Jesus needed the Holy Spirit.' Do you agree with this statement? Make sure you provide evidence to back up your ideas.

7 Why might someone disagree with you? What reasons might they give?

Respond

8 What does the phrase 'For nothing will be impossible with God' mean to you?

WHAT IS THE STORY OF PENTECOST?

One of the opening stories in Acts is the apostles receiving the Holy Spirit at Pentecost. The apostles had gathered to celebrate the Jewish festival of Shavuot, when the Holy Spirit came down and they were transformed from being worried and fearful, to full of confidence and able to spread the word of God.

The story of Pentecost

Luke's Gospel finishes with Jesus' Ascension and the promise that the Holy Spirit will come to the apostles, and this is where Acts of the Apostles continues. Imagine how the apostles and Mary the mother of Jesus must have felt at this point. They had seen Jesus arrested and tried, crucified and risen again before ascending into heaven. Just before ascending, Jesus gave them a mission: they were to continue to spread the Good News and to baptise people who wanted to follow Jesus. The apostles must have wondered how they would manage to do what Jesus had instructed them to do.

In Acts 2:1–12 the story of Pentecost explains what happened next. Many people from many nations had gathered in Jerusalem for Shavuot, a Jewish festival to celebrate the harvest. The apostles had taken themselves away from the crowds of people and locked themselves in a house.

> " 'When the day of Pentecost arrived, they were all together in one place. And suddenly there came from heaven a sound like a mighty rushing wind, and it filled the entire house where they were sitting. And divided tongues of fire appeared to them and rested on each one of them. And they were all filled with the Holy Spirit and began to speak in other tongues as the Spirit gave them utterance.'
>
> *Acts 2:1–4*

▲ The descent of the Holy Spirit on the apostles and Mary at Pentecost *by Elizabeth Wang*

The Holy Spirit appeared in the form of wind and tongues of fire, which came to each of the apostles and Mary. When they received the Holy Spirit, they were changed – they became more confident and could speak in different languages. When we think about what their mission was, we can see how the Holy Spirit was making it possible for them to do what Jesus asked them to do: they had the confidence and the ability to spread the Good News to others.

Telling in our own tongues

The story continues:

> ‘Now there were dwelling in Jerusalem Jews, devout men from every nation under heaven. And at this sound the multitude came together, and they were bewildered because each one was hearing them speak in his own language. And they were amazed and astonished, saying, "Are not all these who are speaking Galileans? And how is it that we hear, each of us in his own native language? Parthians and Medes and Elamites and residents of Mesopotamia, Judea and Cappadocia, Pontus and Asia. Phrygia and Pamphylia, Egypt and the parts of Libya belonging to Cyrene, and visitors from Rome, both Jews and proselytes, Cretans and Arabians – we hear them telling in our own tongues the mighty works of God," And all were amazed and perplexed, saying to one another, "What does this mean?"'
>
> *Acts 2: 5–13*

The apostles come out of hiding and go to the crowds who are amazed and confused by what they're seeing and hearing. How can these Galileans speak so many different languages? The people from different nations who had all gathered in Jerusalem could now hear the Good News in their own language. The Holy Spirit had helped Jesus' apostles to carry out the mission that was given to them.

In the section of scripture that follows, Peter corrects the crowds because some of them think that the apostles are drunk. Peter reminds them that Jesus' life, death and resurrection fulfilled the words of the prophets and that the apostles were filled with the Holy Spirit. According to the story in Acts, three thousand people from the crowd decided that they would like to become a follower of Jesus and so were baptised that day.

Understand

1 What did Jesus promise the apostles before ascending into heaven?
2 What mission did Jesus give to his disciples before ascending into heaven?
3 What two symbols for the Holy Spirit are there in Acts 2:2–3?
4 Identify two ways in which the apostles showed they had been filled with the Holy Spirit.
5 Summarise the events of Pentecost described by St Luke in Acts 2:1–12.
6 What happened after Peter spoke to the crowds at Pentecost?

Discern

7 'Pentecost was only important for the apostles.' Write down arguments to agree and disagree with this statement.

Respond

8 What would your thoughts have been if you had been in the crowds witnessing this event? Write up your thoughts, feelings and emotions as well as any observations or questions you think you might have had.

WHY IS PENTECOST IMPORTANT?

The Holy Spirit didn't just transform the apostles at Pentecost – the Holy Spirit's power led many people to come to have faith in Jesus as the Son of God and to become Christians. This event was important in the history of the Christian faith, as well as being important for Christians today.

The importance of Pentecost

Pentecost was very important since the Holy Spirit enabled the apostles to perform the mission that Jesus had given them. Jesus wanted the apostles to go out into the world, making people disciples and baptising them. When the Holy Spirit came to them, the apostles were given gifts that made it possible for them to fulfil (complete) this mission.

Many Christians refer to Pentecost as the birthday of the Church. The Church teaches that the Church began with Jesus' sacrifice: he gave himself in the first Eucharist at the Last Supper when he says that the bread and wine are his body and blood, broken and poured out for humans, and when he died on the cross. At Pentecost, the Church was first seen by people other than the apostles. At Pentecost the Church began to grow beyond the people who had directly witnessed everything that Jesus had said and done. This is why some Christians call it the beginning, or birthday of the Church.

Jesus' life, death and resurrection were a mission to repair the relationship between God and humans, which humans had broken through sin. The Holy Spirit's mission was to help the apostles to take the message of the Good News of God's love to others. When the Church was formed of people who loved God the Father, who followed Jesus and were filled with the Holy Spirit, these missions were fulfilled and so the Catechism teaches that:

> 'The mission of Christ and the Holy Spirit is brought to completion in the Church.'
>
> *Catechism of the Catholic Church 737*

What happened after Pentecost?

As the book of Acts unfolds, it shows that building up the community of the Church wasn't always easy. The early Christian community was persecuted, meaning that they were treated badly for their faith in Jesus. The Holy Spirit strengthened them to continue.

The early members of the Church community had mainly been Jewish. They changed their lives to follow Jesus' teaching because they came to believe that Jesus was the Messiah. However, gentiles or non-Jews had not yet become members of the Church. In Acts 10 we read of Peter receiving a vision from God which helped him to understand that God has no favourites, and that all those who love God are accepted by God.

> 66 'So Peter opened his mouth and said: "Truly I understand that God shows no particularity, but in every nation anyone who fears him and does what is right is acceptable to him."'
>
> *Acts 10:34*

As Peter preached about this and the faith that Christians have in Jesus, the Holy Spirit came to Peter and all those who were listening. There were gentiles in the crowd and when they received the Holy Spirit, they began to praise God, speaking in different languages, just like the events at Pentecost. Peter baptised the gentiles as Christians as they had received the Holy Spirit and now had faith in Jesus – this meant that the Church grew even more.

▼ *Some Christians today continue the work of the apostles' mission to spread the Good News; Father Henry (on the right in the photo) works for Missio, the Pope's charity for world mission; he supports Christian communities in remote villages throughout rural Malawi, ensuring that Catholics in these areas have access to the sacraments, can grow in faith, and feel part of God's global Church family*

Understand

1 What mission did the apostles have?

2 How did the Holy Spirit help the apostles to fulfil their mission?

3 What makes Pentecost seem like the 'birthday of the Church'?

4 What were the missions of Christ and the Holy Spirit?

5 How does the Church bring these missions to completion?

Discern

6 'Christians should make sure that they celebrate Pentecost.' Do you agree? Give reasons for your opinion.

Respond

7 What does it mean to you to hear that God has no favourites?

WHAT DOES THE CHURCH TEACH ABOUT THE HOLY SPIRIT?

In order that Catholics understand the importance of the Holy Spirit, the Catholic Church gives clear teaching about who the Holy Spirit is, the role of the Holy Spirit and the place of the Holy Spirit as one of the persons of the Trinity. This comes in part through the Nicene Creed, the declaration of faith for Catholics.

What does the Nicene Creed say about the Holy Spirit?

Article 8 of the Nicene Creed sets out some key beliefs about the Holy Spirit, to help Christians to understand the Holy Spirit better:

> " ‖ 'I believe in the Holy Spirit, the Lord, the giver of life'

This statement expresses that Catholics believe that the Holy Spirit exists. By calling the Holy Spirit 'the Lord', Catholics are saying that the Holy Spirit is God.

The idea of the Holy Spirit being the 'giver of life' comes from many teachings through the Bible. In Genesis 1:2 'the Spirit of God was hovering over the face of the waters' just before God began creation. In Genesis 2:7 God is shown breathing life into man. The Hebrew word for this is ***ruah*** which means 'Spirit' and so God's Spirit brought man to life. In the first chapter of Luke's Gospel, when Mary is told that she has been chosen as the mother of Jesus, she is told that Jesus will be conceived through the Holy Spirit bringing God's Son to birth in the flesh. Catholics believe then that all life depends on the Holy Spirit.

> " ‖ 'who proceeds from the Father and the Son, who with the Father and the Son is adored and glorified'

This statement expresses the Catholic belief that the Holy Spirit is one of the three persons of the Holy Trinity. Catholics believe that there is one God who is a trinity of persons: the Father, the Son and the Holy Spirit. It shows that the Holy Spirit is also God. This means it is right for Catholics to pray to (adore and glorify) the Holy Spirit, with the Father and with the Son (Jesus), as all are God.

> " ‖ 'who has spoken through the prophets'

This statement expresses the Catholic belief that the Holy Spirit inspires people to speak God's word to others. Prophets are people called by God to teach others using God's word; these teachings then formed the Bible.

Link

Read more about Arianism and the creation of the Nicene Creed on pages 76–77.

▼ *A painting of Mary and the baby Jesus; Christians believe that the Holy Spirit made the miracle of Jesus' birth possible*

Many of the prophets who spoke God's word are found in the Old Testament. Prophets such as Amos who reminded people of the need for justice, Elijah who challenged people who didn't believe in the one God and Isaiah who foretold the coming of the Messiah, were all guided by the Holy Spirit to give teaching that is still relevant for Christians today.

The New Testament also contains prophets such as John the Baptist, who prepared people for Jesus' life on earth, and Anna, who recognised that Jesus was the Messiah. Many of Jesus' followers and the leaders of the early Church were also guided by the Holy Spirit to continue what Jesus had started on earth.

How the Church explains that the Holy Spirit is God

The Catechism teaches that the Holy Spirit was 'at work with the Father and the Son from the beginning' (CCC 686). The Creed reflects this, explaining that the Holy Spirit:

- is present with the Father and the Son before God's acts of creation
- has acted through the whole story of the Bible
- still guides Catholics today.

Together, these beliefs make it clear that the Holy Spirit is completely God.

In his letter to the Galatians, St Paul explained to Christians that the Holy Spirit lives within them as a sign that they are God's children.

> This means that those who have faith in Jesus are God's children, adopted by God because they have become part of Christ's body, the Church.

> This refers to the Holy Spirit, which St Paul says God puts into a person's heart, helping to guide them as a child of God.

> " 'And because you are sons, God has sent the Spirit of his Son into our hearts, crying "Abba! Father!"'   *Galatians 4:6*

> 'Abba' is an Aramaic word, an affectionate term for 'father' showing that God's children share a strong and close bond with their heavenly father.

Notice the words 'God', 'Spirit' and 'Son' in this Bible quotation. St Paul makes it clear that God is 'Father', 'Son' and 'Spirit'. The Trinity is essential to saving Christians from sin. God the Father who wants to bring salvation, sends the Son to live and die to make salvation possible and sends the Spirit so that people can live as God calls them to do. By showing the activity of the Trinity, St Paul makes it clear that the Holy Spirit is God.

Christian prayer is Trinitarian, meaning that prayer is a relationship with the whole of the Trinity. When Catholics pray, they often do this 'In the name of the Father, and of the Son and of the Holy Spirit.' Catholics believe that they pray to God the Father, in the Son and by the Holy Spirit. This means that the Holy Spirit unites them to the Son, Jesus, by making them part of his body and that when Catholics pray, they pray with Jesus who invites all people to call God 'Father.'

Understand

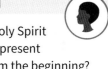

1 How is the Holy Spirit shown to be present with God from the beginning?

2 Identify one way in which the Bible shows that the Holy Spirit is the 'giver of life', as stated in the Nicene Creed.

3 What does it mean to say the Holy Spirit 'proceeds from the Father and the Son'?

4 How does Article 8 of the Nicene Creed help Catholics to understand that the Holy Spirit is God?

5 How does Galatians 4:6 help Catholics to understand that the Holy Spirit is God?

6 Give one Old Testament example of how the Holy Spirit has spoken through the prophets.

7 Give one New Testament example of how the Holy Spirit has spoken through the prophets.

Discern

8 'Believing in the Holy Spirit is not necessary if you believe in God.' What do you think? Give arguments for and against this viewpoint.

Respond

9 Catholics believe the Holy Spirit guides the prophets to speak God's word to others. What issues do you think might need the Holy Spirit's help in today's world?

WHAT IS THE CHURCH?

You have seen that the Church is the community of Jesus' followers. In the Nicene Creed (Article 9), Christians state that they believe in the holy catholic Church and the communion of saints. These teachings convey the belief that the Church is a community open to all people who worship Jesus and that this community is made up of all Christians – those who are alive and those who have already died.

The People of God (CCC 781–786)

The Church was originally made up of Jews and gentiles who had been baptised because they had faith in Jesus and were filled with the Holy Spirit. The Catechism makes it clear that the Church is the **People of God** – a special nation or community. They are unlike any other nation because:

- God has united the members of this community
- membership is given through faith in Jesus and the Sacrament of Baptism
- Jesus is the head of the community and the Holy Spirit flows from him to the people
- the members of the community are God's sons and daughters and have dignity and worth
- its law is Jesus' commandment to 'Love one another. As I have loved you, so you must love one another' (John 13:34)
- the mission of the Church is to help to keep God's truth and to show God's love through the ways in which the members live their lives, by being compassionate and forgiving, for example. The Church needs to show people the way to salvation, which is being saved from sin
- the Church is working towards building God's Kingdom on earth ready for the end of times when God will complete this work.

According to the Catechism, everyone who has faith in Jesus and has been baptised into the Church has three roles: priest, prophet and king.

- Being a priest means to serve God and others. Jesus showed that loving our neighbour is a sacrifice and so being a priest is loving and serving God and putting others first.
- Being a prophet means to share God's word with others, through the things that a person says and the actions that they perform.
- Being a king means to help to build up the Kingdom of God by bringing goodness to the world, and by leading in the Church and the world to bring about God's reign.

Christians believe that Jesus is the perfect priest, prophet and king and so they must follow him in their lives.

The Body of Christ (CCC 787–796)

During Jesus' earthly life his followers were able to see how he acted and learn from his words and actions. This helped them to have faith in Jesus and to share this faith

Useful vocabulary

People of God: one of the names of the Church, emphasising the whole community of believers, united by their belief in God, the Father, Son and Holy Spirit

Body of Christ: one of the names of the Church, emphasising the community of all those who are members of Christ's body through Baptism, with Jesus as their head, working together like one body

Temple of the Holy Spirit: one of the names of the Church, emphasising the community of all those who are led by God's spirit in their lives, given to them through the sacraments

with other people. Christians believe that after Jesus ascended into heaven, the Church is his body on earth, meaning that the Church must act and speak like Jesus in the world. The Holy Spirit helps the Church to do this.

This idea of the Church as the **Body of Christ** helps Christians to understand that they are all united together, and that the role that each individual part of the body plays is really important. Christians believe that Jesus is the head of the body, which means:

- The Holy Spirit flows from Jesus, guiding and helping the whole community.
- Jesus leads the whole Church.
- All people are united to Jesus, in particular through receiving Jesus' body in communion.
- Jesus provides for the Church, which helps the Church grow closer to him.

No-one in the Church is perfect, but by being in the Church and filled with the Holy Spirit, everyone can grow closer to Jesus. The different members of the Church can encourage each other to become closer to God and one another, and the teachings of the Church and the sacraments can help members of the Church to live in the way that makes them followers of Jesus.

▲ *A volunteer working at a soup kitchen; Catholics believe being part of the Church means helping others in every part of their lives, as Jesus would*

The Temple of the Holy Spirit (CCC 797–799)

In the Old Testament, the Temple was the place where God was present on earth in the Holy of Holies, however, the **Temple of the Holy Spirit** isn't talking about a church building. It's talking about the whole community of the Church being a living, breathing worship of God. The Holy Spirit comes from the Father through Jesus: the head of the Church, and flows to the body of the Church: the members. The Holy Spirit is present in Baptism, and the other sacraments, in the virtues or good qualities that the Church teaches and in the goodness of the lives of the members of the Church. The Holy Spirit lives in all of the members of the Church and the ways that they live out their faith.

How do these descriptions of the Church link to the doctrine of the Trinity?

Describing the Church as the People of **God**, the Body of **Christ** and the Temple of the **Holy Spirit**, shows the connection between the Church and the doctrine of the Holy Trinity. Catholics believe each person of the Trinity lives through the Church and unites humans with God, the Father, Son and Holy Spirit.

Discern

7 'The Church can't be the Body of Christ, it is full of sinners.' What would a Catholic say about this idea? Why might someone disagree?

Understand

1 Why are there different descriptions of the Church?
2 Give two reasons why the Church as the 'People of God' is unlike any other nation.
3 Explain what Christians believe about being a priest, prophet and king.
4 What does the belief about the Church as the Body of Christ teach about the relationship of Christians to Jesus?
5 How is the Church the Temple of the Holy Spirit?
6 What is the connection between these descriptions of the Church and the Holy Trinity?

Respond

8 Which of these descriptions do you think best describes the Church, based on your experience of the Church? Explain your answer.

WHAT IS THE SACRAMENT OF CONFIRMATION?

Sacraments are sacred rites which make God's invisible saving power visible and present to those who receive them. Through the sacraments, God's saving power transforms a person. The Sacrament of Confirmation is when a person is strengthened by the Holy Spirit so that they can live out their vocation: their calling to follow God. The preparation, celebration and meaning of this sacrament are all important for Catholics as it often marks the independent decision of a person to deepen their commitment to their faith.

What is Confirmation?

Confirmation is one of the Sacraments of Initiation, alongside Baptism and the Eucharist. Initiation means becoming a member of something and so when these three sacraments have been celebrated, a person is a full member of the Church. In the UK, Confirmation is often celebrated by teenagers, but it can be a celebrated as early as age seven, or much later in life.

Confirmation can be traced back to the story of Pentecost in Acts 2:1–12 where the Holy Spirit empowered Jesus' apostles. While we may find connections between Confirmation and Pentecost, we see even closer links with Acts 19:5–6 which describes people being baptised first, then as Paul lays his hands on them they are filled with the Holy Spirit.

How does a person prepare for Confirmation?

Preparation for Confirmation is taken seriously, since the sacrament itself is an important commitment. A candidate for Confirmation will attend catechesis, or Confirmation classes, where they will learn more about the Catholic faith, and the importance of the Sacrament of Confirmation.

The candidate will choose a sponsor – someone who will be by their side as they are confirmed and who will support them in their faith journey. The sponsor can be the candidate's **godparent**, but can also be another person who lives a faithful Catholic life.

The candidate can also choose a Confirmation name. This is usually the name of a saint who inspires the candidate. This might be because of how they expressed their faith or because they have particular qualities that the candidate would like to develop too.

Useful vocabulary

godparent: a practising Catholic, chosen to help nurture the faith of a person being baptised

What happens at Confirmation?

Usually the bishop confers (gives) Confirmation. The sacrament happens during Mass. Following the Gospel reading, the candidates for Confirmation are called forward. They renew their baptismal promises. These promises are to reject sin and to have faith in God and the Church. If the candidate was baptised as a small child, these promises would have been made on the candidate's behalf, so it's important that the candidate now makes these promises themselves to show they understand them and are choosing the path of faith for themselves.

Each candidate then kneels or stands in front of the bishop, who calls them by their Confirmation name. Laying hands on the candidate is a symbol of the Holy Spirit. The candidate's sponsor will place their right hand on the candidate's shoulder and the bishop lays his hands on the candidate's head. This is to bring the power and blessings of the Holy Spirit to the candidate.

▲ *A candidate is confirmed by the bishop, who anoints her with the oil of chrism*

The bishop then anoints or blesses the candidate with another symbol of the Holy Spirit, chrism oil, by placing the oil in the sign of the cross on the candidate's forehead. Anointing with chrism oil shows that the candidate has been called by God and given a vocation by God.

The bishop says 'be sealed with the Gift of the Holy Spirit'. The candidate replies 'Amen.'

The bishop then says 'peace be with you' and the candidate replies 'And with your spirit.'

Understand

1. What type of sacrament is the Sacrament of Confirmation?
2. Identify three ways in which a candidate prepares for Confirmation.
3. What are the baptismal promises renewed in Confirmation?
4. What does it mean when the bishop lays his hands on the candidate's head?
5. What does it mean when the bishop anoints the candidate with chrism oil?
6. Explain the connection between Pentecost and Confirmation.

Discern

7. 'Catholics don't need to be confirmed.' Why would a Catholic disagree with this view? Why might someone agree with it?

Respond

8. **Either:** Have you been confirmed or are you preparing to be confirmed? Write down why this sacrament is important to you.
   Or:
   What qualities would you like to develop as you become more mature?

WHY IS THE SACRAMENT OF CONFIRMATION IMPORTANT?

Receiving the Sacrament of Confirmation is important in the life of a Catholic, no matter when they celebrate this sacrament. Through this sacrament, the candidate is sealed with the **gifts of the Holy Spirit**, which helps each candidate to live as God calls them to.

The gifts of the Holy Spirit

Catholics believe that the Holy Spirit helps people to grow in holiness, by helping them to become closer to God. The Holy Spirit does this through giving gifts to a Catholic at Baptism and strengthening these gifts at Confirmation. They are called 'gifts' because they are freely given by the Holy Spirit though love. The Holy Spirit's gifts are named in the Bible:

▲ *Catholics believe that the Holy Spirit gives people gifts, such as knowledge, to help them grow in holiness*

> " 'the Spirit of **wisdom** and **understanding**, the Spirit of **counsel** and **might**, the Spirit of **knowledge** and **fear of the Lord**. And his delight shall be in the fear of the LORD.'
>
> *Isaiah 11:2–3*

What do these gifts mean?

Wisdom	The ability to make the right choices, applying God's word to difficult situations in life.
Understanding	To rightly interpret and understand what God is revealing.
Counsel	To allow God to guide oneself, helping a person to gain salvation.
Fortitude (might)	To be set on doing what is right and overcoming difficult obstacles in order to be close to God.
Knowledge	The ability to study, learn and remember what God has revealed.
Piety	Deep respect for God, and all that God has made. Living a life of holiness and striving not to sin.
Fear of the Lord	Living one's whole life for God, showing God reverence and awe in all that is done, and relying on God alone.

Useful vocabulary

gifts of the Holy Spirit: seven spiritual gifts given by the Holy Spirit during the Sacrament of Confirmation: wisdom, understanding, counsel, might, knowledge, piety and fear of the Lord

fruits of the Spirit: the behaviours and attitudes that are shown by a person who is filled with the Holy Spirit, such as love, joy and kindness

Catholics believe that these gifts help them to live the life that God calls them to. St John Henry Newman (1801–1890) described this as 'some definite service' meaning that we all have a particular way to serve God in our lives.

Just as the apostles were able to fulfil their mission when the Holy Spirit empowered them at Pentecost, Catholics believe that the Holy Spirit continues to guide individuals so that they can live out their own mission. In the Youth Catechism is says:

> 'The Holy Spirit builds up the Church and impels her. He reminds her of her mission. He calls people into her service and sends the necessary gifts. He leads us ever deeper into communion with the Triune God.'
>
> *Youth Catechism 119*

This means that the Holy Spirit helps the whole Church and individuals in the Church to follow God by giving leadership and direction, as well as the gifts that people need to be able to do what God has called them to do.

St Paul referred to this in his first letter to the Corinthians where he taught:

> 'there are varieties of gifts, but the same Spirit; and there are varieties of service, but the same Lord; and there are varieties of activities, but it is the same God who empowers them all in everyone.'
>
> *1 Corinthians 12:4*

The fruits of the Holy Spirit

There are twelve **fruits of the Spirit**. In Galatians 5:22 Paul names nine: love, joy, peace, patience, kindness, generosity, faithfulness, gentleness and self-control. The other fruits of the Spirit are goodness, modesty and chastity. Catholics believe that these fruits come from the Holy Spirit, who is God, and so they help Catholics to know some of God's qualities. This helps them to see how to live, to be closer to God.

When the gifts of the Holy Spirit are given to a person, they should work to use them well, so that they can 'bear fruit' and show these qualities themselves. As a person becomes closer to God and more holy, the fruits of the Spirit are more clearly shown in in their lives.

Catholics believe that the gifts and the fruits of the Holy Spirit help them to become the person that God has created them to be. They can't always do this on their own and need God's help. Both the gifts and fruits of the Holy Spirit remind Catholics that while they might feel that they are wise or joyful, the wisdom and joy that comes from God is far greater than any human could achieve on their own.

Understand

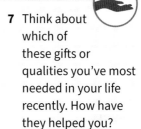

1 When are the gifts of the Holy Spirit given, and when are they strengthened?
2 Why are the gifts of the Holy Spirit called gifts?
3 Name the gifts of the Holy Spirit
4 Name the fruits of the Holy Spirit.
5 What is different about the wisdom or joy that comes from God?

Link

Read more about the gifts and fruits of the Spirit on pages 144–145.

Discern

6 'We can develop good qualities without God's help.' Give arguments for and against this viewpoint.

Respond

7 Think about which of these gifts or qualities you've most needed in your life recently. How have they helped you?

8 What particular gifts do you think you have? What do you think your particular definite service is to the Church or to the world?

HOW SHOULD WE LIVE?

Christians believe that people who are filled with the Holy Spirit show this through the good things they do in the world. This positive behaviour reflects the fruits of the Spirit. Christians also believe that when a person doesn't allow the Holy Spirit to guide them, this can also be seen in their lives, as they give in to temptation and show poor behaviour or weak choices.

The works of the flesh and the fruits of the Spirit

In Galatians 5, we read St Paul's letter to the Churches in Galatia. His letter, like all of his letters, aimed to help the community to understand the Christian faith better, and to encourage new Christians in their faith. In Galatians 5, St Paul talks about two kinds of behaviours or attitudes: the **works of the flesh** and the fruits of the Spirit.

Catholics believe that ever since humans gave in to temptation in the Garden of Eden, they have lived in sin. The works of the flesh are temptations that human beings face every day in our world, for example:

> '... enmity, strife, jealousy, fits of anger, rivalries, dissensions, divisions, envy.'
>
> *Galatians 5:20–21*

These behaviours and attitudes are natural human weaknesses – it is often easier to show anger or to be greedy, or to care more about things than people, but Catholics see this behaviour as sinful. St Paul warns that a person who commits these sins cannot be part of God's Kingdom. However, St Paul offers Christians hope and explains that they can find help through the Holy Spirit:

> 'But I say, **walk by the Spirit**, and you will not gratify the desires of the flesh.'
>
> *Galatians 5:16*

This means that if a person allows themselves to be led by the Holy Spirit, they will not give in to human weaknesses in the works of the flesh. The way to do this is to show the fruits of the Spirit in the way they live. These are:

- love
- joy
- peace
- patience
- kindness
- goodness
- faithfulness
- gentleness
- self-control.

The Catechism includes generosity, modesty and chastity.

What does this mean for Christians today?

In order to walk by the Spirit, Christians will ask God's guidance through prayer, read the Bible and consider the example of Jesus. The Youth Catechism teaches that an individual can find help by listening quietly to their conscience. It describes

Useful vocabulary

works of the flesh: human temptations or weaknesses such as jealousy, anger and envy

Link

Read more about the gifts and fruits of the Spirit on pages 142–143.

the presence of the Holy Spirit within each person as 'the quiet guest of our soul' (YC 120). Using this help, Christians can then draw on the gifts of the Holy Spirit to try to make good choices and to live a life that shows the fruits of the Spirit.

But even with God's guidance, this is not always an easy thing to do. Our modern world is full of temptation and many people feel pressure to act in a certain way. We are bombarded with information on social media, in magazines and on TV. We are constantly updated on the latest trends and told what we should be wearing or listening to. This fast-paced environment, where we're encouraged to have and want new things all the time, can make it challenging to show patience and self-control.

▲ Social media can be used for good but doesn't always encourage us to behave in a kind and generous way

We may also feel we have good reasons to not show behaviours such as love, gentleness and peace when we see violence in the world and crimes against innocent or vulnerable people. Many young people experience bullying or intimidation: is it wrong to feel angry or vengeful when this happens?

While it is natural to feel these things, Catholics believe that Jesus teaches them it is not right to act on these feelings. In Luke's Gospel, Jesus commands his followers to 'Love your enemies, do good to those who hate you' (Luke 6:27). Catholics therefore use the fruits of the Spirit to help direct their behaviour away from selfishness or anger. They might try to consciously cherish the things they already have, or put themselves in someone else's shoes to understand why a person acts as a bully.

In Galatians 6, St Paul talks about the importance of supporting one another. He tells Christians to:

❝ ‖ 'Bear one another's burdens, and so fulfil the law of Christ.'

Galatians 6:2

Catholics believe they should look out for each other and help others to make the right choices in life, because it's not easy to do so alone. The Holy Spirit is present in the community of the Church, so by helping one another Catholics believe they are not only welcoming the Holy Spirit into themselves, they are strengthening the whole Church of which the Holy Spirit is a part.

Understand

1 What are the two behaviours or attitudes that St Paul writes about in Galatians 5?
2 What is the difference between the two behaviours?
3 What does St Paul warn about the works of the flesh?
4 In your own words, explain the advice St Paul gives in Galatians 5:16.
5 Name three things Catholics can do today to walk by the Spirit.

Discern

6 Is there ever a good reason not to follow the fruits of the Spirit? What might a Catholic say? Why might someone disagree with this?

7 'Social media leads to envy and jealousy.' Write an argument that agrees and one that disagrees with this statement. Think about how a Catholic might respond and use the fruits of the Spirit in your answer.

Respond

8 Look at the fruits of the Spirit. Think of a time that you demonstrated these positive qualities recently and explain how it made you feel.

HOW IS PENTECOST SHOWN THROUGH ART?

OBJECTIVES

In this lesson you will compare and contrast **two pieces of art that show Pentecost.**

Art has been used throughout history to depict stories from the Bible, not only because art helps to communicate the meaning of Bible stories but also because it can help people to deepen their understanding of these stories. The story of Pentecost is very dramatic, so it has inspired many pieces of artwork.

Life of Jesus Mafa: Pentecost

Pentecost is from a series of paintings about Jesus' life. The pictures were painted in the 1970s to teach about Jesus in Northern Cameroon, in Africa. A Catholic priest called Father François Vidil worked with theologians, an artist and members of the Mafa Christian community to create paintings of Jesus shown as a Black African man. He hoped that through doing this, the stories about Jesus from the Bible would be more meaningful for Black African communities.

Link

Read about another artwork from the *Life of Jesus Mafa* series on pages 120–121.

There is fire, not only a large flame in the middle of the group, but individual flames over people's heads. Fire is one of the symbols of the Holy Spirit.

This man's clothing is being moved by the wind. The wind is another symbol of the Holy Spirit.

The people gathered are the apostles of Jesus, and Mary the mother of Jesus.

The descent of the Holy Spirit on the apostles and Mary at Pentecost by Elizabeth Wang

Elizabeth Wang (1942–2016) was an artist who became a Catholic when she was 26. Her faith was very important to her and was clearly seen in her artwork. Some of her paintings were inspired by visions that she received when she was praying. She used art to communicate teachings of Jesus and the Church.

On page 133 you can see a painting she made about Pentecost. It is very simple but very effective. At the bottom of the image, she shows Mary and the disciples. The light of the Holy Spirit is coming from the heavens and every head has a flame upon it. The flames on each person's head are moving up towards heaven.

Light is an important feature in all of Elizabeth Wang's paintings. In this painting, the light is showing the holiness that radiates from the Holy Spirit.

> Look at the image on page 133. Do you notice:
> - The figure in pale blue in the centre? Perhaps this emphasises Mary's special role.
> - The flame on the central figure is joined to the flame in the centre of the page. Is this showing Mary's special connection with God as the mother of Jesus?
> - The figures are still but the flames are full of movement and life.

There is joy and confusion on people's faces. Someone is covering their eyes. Is the light blinding or are they taking time to consider what's happening? Two men are supporting each other: do they feel a little overwhelmed?

Mary and the man next to her have their arms outstretched in a prayerful gesture. They look like they're welcoming the Holy Spirit and are excited by what is happening.

Understand

1 Identify two reasons why art is used to communicate Bible stories.
2 Why was the *Life of Jesus Mafa* series of paintings created?
3 What did Wang use art to do?
4 Write a description of Wang's painting.
5 Which symbol of the Holy Spirit is seen in both pieces of art?

Discern

6 What Catholic idea about the Holy Spirit do you think stands out most from the *Life of Jesus Mafa: Pentecost*. Does Elizabeth Wang's painting explore ideas about the Holy Spirit in a similar or different way?
7 Which painting do you think better helps you to understand Pentecost? Give reasons for your opinion.

Respond

8 Why do you think it's important that different communities have their own ways of showing Bible stories? Think about Bible story pictures you may have seen while growing up. How did that artwork make you feel?

HOW IS PENTECOST CELEBRATED IN DIFFERENT COUNTRIES?

Pentecost is an important celebration for Christians, but the ways Christians celebrate differ around the world. Some simply take part in special worship at Mass, where other groups go beyond what happens in church to continue the celebrations in their community.

Celebrations of Pentecost in church

Pentecost is celebrated to remember the giving of the Holy Spirit to the apostles, and Mary the mother of Jesus. On this day Mary and the apostles had gathered away from the large crowds of people who had come to Jerusalem for the harvest festival. The Holy Spirit descended on their group, giving them the gifts to preach to the crowds, meaning that many people became Christian on that day.

Catholic Churches celebrate Pentecost in their services of Mass on a Sunday. It is celebrated on the fiftieth day (seventh Sunday) after Easter Sunday. Sometimes the celebration is called Whitsunday or White Sunday. This name probably came from the ancient custom of new Catholics (baptised at Easter, or in some cases, on the evening before Pentecost) wearing white robes to show their new life as Christians.

Priests will usually wear red vestments to symbolise the tongues of fire that came to the disciples. The congregation will hear the story of the Pentecost from Acts 2 and the priest will preach about the importance of the Holy Spirit.

Celebrations of Pentecost in local communities

Parish communities might take Pentecost as a chance to celebrate the different communities that members of the Church belong to. For example, they may have different languages spoken during the Mass or share food from around the world after Mass. As it's considered to be the birthday of the Church, many parishes will have some kind of celebration.

Pilgrimage is also an important part of Pentecost celebrations in many different countries. Pilgrimages can be joyful events, but also allow time for quiet, spiritual reflection. In Germany, some Catholics ride a pilgrimage on horseback in the Bavarian Forest. In Hungary, up to 100,000 pilgrims travel to Csíksomlyó in Transylvania to pray before a statue of the Virgin Mary. The Chartres pilgrimage in France involves around 20,000 Catholics from over 30 countries. For three days they walk from the Cathedral of Notre Dame in Paris to the Cathedral of Notre Dame in Chartres. This pilgrimage

Useful vocabulary

pilgrimage: a journey made for a spiritual purpose

▲ *At Pentecost, priests will usually wear red vestments to symbolise the tongues of fire that came to the disciples*

has inspired Christian charities to organise Pentecost pilgrimages in Iraq, Lebanon and Egypt. Catholics believe that Pentecost pilgrimages are important because they:

- allow the Holy Spirit to guide them, as it did the apostles and Mary
- gather nations together, to reflect the gathered people in Jerusalem
- allow Catholics to take the Good News to others, as the apostles did at Pentecost.

Italy: *Pascha Rosatum*

In Italy, the celebration of Pentecost is sometimes called *Pascha Rosatum* or 'Rose Sunday'. This is because it is the custom of churches to scatter the petals of red roses from the ceilings of the church to symbolise the tongues of fire that came down upon the disciples. One famous place where this happens is the Pantheon, an ancient Catholic church in Rome. It is believed to be a tradition that goes back to AD 609 when the Pantheon became a Christian place of worship. While the *Veni Creator Spiritus* (Come, Creator Spirit) is sung, thousands of rose petals are dropped down the large opening at the top of the dome, landing on the people beneath.

Poland: Green Holiday

As well as going to Mass on Pentecost, Polish people might decorate their homes with greenery – traditionally birch branches with leaves on them. This is where the name 'Green Holiday' comes from. This action is done in the hope that God's blessing will come to the homes and families of those who put this greenery out. In the past, there also would be a procession to the fields to bless crops, and animals such as cows may have their horns decorated with garlands of greenery and flowers.

The origins of the celebration of the greenery comes from a time before Christianity when spring was celebrated and nature seemed to be re-born from the winter. The rituals were carried out in the hope communities would be blessed with fertility and good crops later in the year. However, now they are important symbols of God blessing the world just as the early Church was blessed by the Holy Spirit.

Some churches lower a carved dove over the congregation. This is called 'swinging the Holy Ghost (Spirit)' and is a reminder of the Holy Spirit coming to the apostles.

▲ Rose petals being dropped from the ceiling of the Pantheon in Rome at Pentecost (also known as 'Pascha Rosatum' or 'Rose Sunday')

Discern

6 Celebrations of Pentecost around the world can express Catholic beliefs about the Holy Spirit – for example, the Pentecost story is shared and explained. They can also express the culture and traditions of different communities – for example, it is the custom of Italian churches to scatter red rose petals, and in Poland Catholics decorate their home with birch branches. Which do you think is more important, expressing beliefs, culture or both? Explain your view.

Understand

1 When is Pentecost celebrated in the Church?
2 Where does the name 'Whitsunday' come from?
3 Why does a priest wear red vestments on Pentecost?
4 Why are red rose petals used to celebrate Pentecost in Italy?
5 Why are green branches put into people's homes for Pentecost in Poland?

Respond

7 Which of these celebrations would you like to see or experience personally?

ASSESSMENT

Key vocabulary

Write a definition for these key terms.

Holy Spirit	Pentecost	*ruah*	People of God
Body of Christ	Temple of the Holy Spirit	Confirmation	fruits of the Spirit

Knowledge check

1 Which of these symbols of the Holy Spirit are named in Acts 2:1–12?

    a dove and flames

    b wind and flames

    c dove and wind

2 Who was the author of Acts of the Apostles?

3 Copy out and complete the following:

    Catholics believe that the H................. S................. is the third person of the T.............. .

4 What is the name of the sacrament where a person is sealed by the gifts of the Holy Spirit?

5 What could the apostles do when they had received the Holy Spirit at Pentecost?

6 What is a vocation?

7 Name four fruits of the Holy Spirit.

8 Explain what it means to describe the Church as the Body of Christ.

9 Describe the things Jesus said that the Spirit of the Lord would help him to do.

10 Explain how the Holy Spirit helped the early Christian community.

TIP

Think about what it means to be 'sealed'. What gifts could do this?

TIP

Look back at pages 138–139. Consider how the parts of a body are connected – what does that suggest about the Church?

Extended writing activity

This assessment is for you to show what you have learned in this chapter and to develop your extended writing skills. Here is a big question:

Why is the Holy Spirit important to Christians? How might a Christian show its importance in how they express their beliefs?

This can be broken down into two smaller questions. Your teacher will direct you to which questions they want you to answer.

1 **What are the different ways the Holy Spirit is important to Christians?**

Make a list of ideas or examples to help you answer this question. Here are some to get you started:

The Holy Spirit is important to Christians because it...
- is active in the Church today
- was promised by Jesus
- helped the early Church
- is present in the sacraments.

Now write one or two paragraphs to try to expand on your chosen points.

Here is an example:

The Holy Spirit is important to Christians because it gives them gifts that help them to follow God. For example, at Pentecost the Holy Spirit ○......... gave the apostles the confidence to spread the Good News and the languages to be able to speak to the crowds of people. This was important since, when people heard the News, they became Christians too – many people were baptised that day and lots of Christians call Pentecost the birthday of the Church.

Words you could use:

Good News   gifts   languages   Pentecost

2 **How might Christians express this?**

Try to write two more paragraphs about how Christians might express their belief in the importance of the Holy Spirit. You'll need to consider the different ways that Christians show the importance of the Holy Spirit in their own lives, their community or in the life of the Church.

Examples you could use:

Mass   Confirmation   Catholic mission

TIP

- There is a lot you could include here. The big challenge is to decide what you are going to write about. It's better to write in detail about two or three ideas, than to write very briefly about lots of different ideas.

- Really good answers will include specific information about the Holy Spirit, specialist vocabulary and evidence that you understand this information yourself.

It's a good idea to refer to **religious teachings** in your answer. Here, the student has backed up their point using a Bible story.

TIP

In your answer you need to try to make a point – so one way in which Christians express that the Holy Spirit is important – and then back it up with relevant examples or explanations. You could refer to beliefs and teachings, actions, liturgy and traditions.

CHAPTER 6:

DIALOGUE AND ENCOUNTER

Introduction

Have you ever wondered why there are so many different Christian Churches in the world and what caused them all to develop?

Christianity is the largest religion in the world, with around 2.3 billion people today identifying as Christian. A Christian is defined as someone who believes in and follows the teachings of Jesus Christ, who lived and taught two thousand years ago. Christianity is both a faith and a way of life for many people, but there are many different types of Christians in the world – so how did this happen?

Christianity developed over thousands of years and many questions or problems naturally arose in that time. **Meetings called ecumenical councils were held to try to address these and maintain one united Church.** In this chapter you will look at the first such meeting – **the Council of Jerusalem** – which was held at the time of the apostles. However, like anything that has a long history, there were times when disagreements on matters of faith and practice could not be resolved. This led to divides and reforms within Christianity, meaning that different Churches, or denominations, formed. **One of the biggest splits in the history of the Church followed from the Protestant Reformation** that took place in Western Europe in the sixteenth century.

Today, there are many different Christian denominations. Each one holds particular Christian beliefs and practises the Christian faith in different ways, but **all are united as branches of Christianity, with faith and love of Jesus**. The Catholic Church teaches that, despite any differences, Christians should make it a goal to remember the beliefs that unite them, and to work together to bring about the kind of society that Jesus wanted, where all people have what they need to thrive regardless of their faith and background.

This chapter explores the development of the Catholic Church and how it engages with other Christian denominations. At school, you will also learn about other world religions and study how those faiths have a big impact on the lives of their believers. You might explore non-religious worldviews, too. Some of what you will learn in this chapter, about the importance of dialogue between different groups and finding common ground, might also be useful ideas to hold in mind as you encounter and learn about other religions and worldviews, too.

153

HOW HAVE COUNCILS BEEN IMPORTANT IN THE CHURCH?

Over the centuries many important **theological** and moral questions have come up as Christians have tried to live and worship faithfully. Sometimes, the Church has called meetings to answer them, so that Christians would know how to live and act in accordance with the Church and God's law. These meetings began very early on in the history of the Church and continue into the present day.

How did Christianity spread and grow?

Christianity is a religion which began as a movement within Judaism. Eventually, the Jewish disciples of Jesus became known as Christians. The early Christian Church was established due to three main events: the institution of the Eucharist, the **Great Commission** and Pentecost. After his resurrection, Jesus instructed his apostles:

> " 'Go, therefore and make disciples of all nations, baptising them in the name of the Father and of the Son and of the Holy Spirit.'
>
> *Matthew 28:19*

This became known as the Great Commission. In this statement Jesus is instructing his followers to build his Church on earth, so that all people can hear the Good News. Pentecost, often referred to as the birthday of the Church, marks the descent of the Holy Spirit onto the apostles. This gave the apostles the gift of tongues – the ability to speak in many languages. The Bible teaches that the apostles used this gift to preach the Gospel to Jews and gentiles alike, and many joined the Church.

As the first leaders of the Church, the apostles, particularly St Paul, were essential in spreading Christianity. As they spread out to distant lands, St Paul wrote many letters which recorded the growth of the Church in different parts of the ancient Roman world, and some of the disputes that arose in the early Church. These can be found in the New Testament. St Paul helped to establish the Christian Church throughout the Roman Empire, but Christians were heavily persecuted by the Romans until Emperor Constantine converted in AD 312. By this point, the apostles had all died, but their successors had become leaders of the Church as bishops to particular churches. The Church faced many decisions and disputes about the correct way to interpret and practise the Christian faith. This led to conflict in the Church with some groups breaking away.

What is an ecumenical council?

In its early stages, when the Church experienced issues or had theological questions that it needed answering, it called a meeting or a council. These were formal

Useful vocabulary

theological: relating to the study of the nature of God and religious belief

Great Commission: Jesus' instruction to the disciples to spread the Gospel to all nations of the world

ecumenical council: in Catholicism, a meeting of the bishops of the worldwide Church at the invitation of the Pope, to decide on matters of the Church

dogma: an essential belief which becomes a binding teaching in Catholicism

gatherings of the leaders of the Church at the time to give answers on matters of faith, to ensure Church unity. These councils began at the time of the apostles. The first meeting is written about in the Bible and it is known as the Council of Jerusalem. Since the First Council of Nicaea these meetings have been described as **ecumenical councils**, and they continue to be used by the Church today to settle important matters.

An ecumenical council is a meeting of the bishops of the worldwide Church at the invitation of the Pope. The Pope sometimes uses his own authority to make decisions on important questions of belief, but these are usually made by a council of the Church with all the bishops in the world. The bishops, with the Pope, have the authority to outline the teachings of the Church and identify errors which have happened in certain areas. Since the first official ecumenical council in Nicaea in AD 325 there have been 21 councils in total. Councils try to peacefully resolve theological issues and are a way in which the bishops, in union with the Pope, can communicate important beliefs to Church members.

Link

To read more about the Council of Jerusalem, go to page 156.

Link

Read more about the authority of the bishops on pages 52–55.

Councils clarify matters of dogma

As we read on pages 77–78, the First Council of Nicaea was called to clarify the Church's position on the divinity of Jesus. Arius argued that Jesus was not God but, as the Son of God, he was created by God. By stating this, Arius was undermining the core belief of Christianity: the Incarnation. At the First Council of Nicaea, Arianism was debated and the council decided it was incorrect. The council declared that Jesus was God, and of one being (consubstantial) with the Father.

This is an example of **dogma** – an essential belief which becomes a binding teaching in Catholicism. Ecumenical councils meet to debate and then clearly communicate where the Church stands on matters of faith and morals.

▲ *The First Council of Nicaea was called to clarify the Church's position on the divinity of Jesus*

Understand

1 What is an ecumenical council? What is its purpose?
2 Who is present at ecumenical councils?
3 What does the word 'dogma' mean for Catholics?

Discern

4 'Ecumenical councils are not relevant today.' Give one reason to disagree with this statement, giving specific examples to support your point.

Respond

5 Think of a time when you have disagreed with someone. What do you think are good ways to reach an agreement? Is this always possible? What happens when agreement is not possible?

WHAT HAPPENED AT THE COUNCIL OF JERUSALEM?

The apostles were the first Church leaders to call a council to discuss an important matter of Christian faith. This was recorded in the Bible and known as the Council of Jerusalem. The Council of Jerusalem is very important in the Church as it gave some clear answers to problems that the Church was having at the time. It was also the point at which Christianity spread beyond its Jewish origins into the gentile world. This was the start of a long history of councils being used throughout Church history to help ensure a positive way forward when difficulties arose.

What was the Council of Jerusalem?

The early followers of Jesus were Jews. However, as the Church began to expand, many gentiles (people who were not Jewish) started to hear the Good News of Jesus. As all the early followers of Jesus were Jewish, the Church was unsure of what rules gentiles needed to follow. This caused many questions to be asked within the Church from its Jewish members about who a follower of Jesus could be and what this would involve. The growth of the early Church is recorded in the Acts of the Apostles, where we learn that the apostles called the Council of Jerusalem around AD 48 to answer two questions:

- Do gentiles need to become Jews before they can become Christians?
- Do gentiles have to observe Jewish Law after they become Christian?

There are two different accounts of the Council of Jerusalem in Acts 15 and Galatians 3; both accounts clearly state that the answer to these questions was 'no'.

In Acts, St Luke writes that after the apostles and the elders of the Church had debated these issues, St Peter stood and said:

> " 'And God, who knows the heart, bore witness to them, by giving them the Holy Spirit just as he did to us.'
>
> *Acts 15:8*

Here Peter is saying Jews and gentiles are each chosen by God and there is no difference between them, therefore gentiles do not need to become Jews and keep the Jewish Law to be Christian. He goes on to explain that they simply need to refrain from idolatry (worshiping an image as though it were God) and certain types of immorality, and to have faith.

In Galatians, St Paul reinforces this message. He states that 'for in Christ Jesus you are all sons of God, through faith' (Galatians 3:26), which meant that all people become brothers and sisters when they believe in Jesus: earthly differences like

Useful vocabulary

universal Church: the whole community of Catholics in the world

being Jewish or gentile do not matter. Therefore, gentiles did not need to convert to Judaism as they were already true followers of Jesus simply through their faith.

Resolving differences through dialogue

The Council of Jerusalem is the first example of what became known as an ecumenical council because Church leaders at that time gathered to discuss a difficult issue which, if not solved, could have divided the Church. Originally, Peter and Paul disagreed on the issue of gentile Christians with only Paul supporting the acceptance of gentiles into the Church. Through dialogue (discussion and debate) they came to an agreement which they then shared with the followers of the Church. This meant they could move forward in harmony, and that everyone could remain one faith and share the same beliefs. The Council of Jerusalem was very important as it showed the importance of dialogue and listening in arriving at an understanding of what is true and right. Catholics believe that, together, the Church, through listening to all of its members, can arrive at an understanding of what God is asking of them at this time and place.

▲ A stained glass image of the Council of Jerusalem from an Anglican church in Rome

Today, bishops of the Church continue the work of the apostles, including the tradition of using ecumenical councils to meet and resolve issues. Bishops from the **universal Church** gather to clarify what the Church should believe and how it should act, to ensure unity within the Church. The main function of the Council of Jerusalem was to answer the question as to whether Christians needed to be Jews first and to promote unity and peace in the Church. Councils that have followed have also aimed to promote unity and peace. Ecumenical councils therefore are very important as they began at the very founding of the Church and continue up to the present day. The Church continues to use councils as a way of clarifying matters of faith and morals because Christ promised to be with his Church until the end of time. The whole Church has the authority to teach and define the faith and does so through its councils, as well as through the ordinary teaching of its bishops in union with the Pope. In this way the Church remains one, united in the truth.

Most recently, the Second Vatican Council was called by Pope John XXIII in 1962 to concentrate on how the Church was working in the modern world and the ways they needed to change to connect with modern people. They produced many documents to share with the Church such as *Dei Verbum*. Ecumenical councils are the way in which the Church settles disputed matters and communicates the truth for every time and place.

Understand

1 What is a gentile?

2 What was the Council of Jerusalem and why was it called?

3 Where in the New Testament do the two different accounts of the Council of Jerusalem come from?

4 a What did the Council of Jerusalem decide?

   b What impact did this have?

5 How do councils help to resolve problems?

Discern
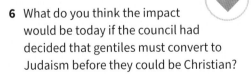

6 What do you think the impact would be today if the council had decided that gentiles must convert to Judaism before they could be Christian?

Respond
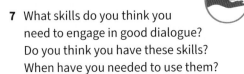

7 What skills do you think you need to engage in good dialogue? Do you think you have these skills? When have you needed to use them?

WHY ARE THERE SO MANY CHRISTIAN DENOMINATIONS?

The Church has faced many challenges and when disagreements between groups have happened the Church has tried to find solutions to keep believers together. However, sometimes disagreements could not be resolved, and this led to a **schism**, or split, where a group would choose to break away from the Church, leading to the creation of a new Christian community, separate from the Catholic Church.

What happens when differences cannot be resolved through dialogue?

We have read about how Arianism caused one of the first divides within the Church, over a difference in opinion about the divinity of Jesus. The First Council of Nicaea was held in AD 325 to debate this issue and it was decided that Arianism was incorrect.

After this council, those who followed Arius and Arianism were exiled (forced to leave and go to another place) by Emperor Constantine because their beliefs were considered to be **heresy**. The Council had not been able to resolve the different ideas that these groups held, so Arian Christians broke away from the main Church. Arian Christianity continued for many years after the council of Nicaea.

Another example of a group who held views that differed from the mainstream were followers of Nestorius, who became known as 'Nestorians'. Nestorians denied the Incarnation, believing that Jesus was a God-inspired man, not God-made-human. The Council of Chalcedon in AD 451 condemned this, stating that Jesus was one person, both fully God and fully human. This resulted in Nestorians breaking away from the Church. There are Churches today which have developed from those groups who broke away in the fifth century.

The Reformation and the Council of Trent

The biggest schism in Western Christianity happened as a result of the Protestant Reformation, which took place in Western Europe in the sixteenth century. Those who called for **reform** were called Protestants, because they protested against the Church. In some parts of Europe, they called for reform because they objected to certain corrupt practices such as the selling of **indulgences**, which people believed they could buy to reduce punishment from sin. In England, this movement combined with King Henry VIII's fallout with the Pope, who would not grant him a divorce. Henry used the Reformation as an excuse to abolish and raid monasteries in England to pay for wars in France. Henry made himself the supreme head of the Church in England instead of the Pope.

Link

To read more about Arianism, go to pages 76–77.

Useful vocabulary

schism: a split or division within a group

heresy: an opinion or belief that goes against Church teaching, or the denial of a revealed truth

reform: to make changes to something

indulgences: a way to reduce the amount of punishment given for sin

Martin Luther was a key figure in the Reformation who spoke out against the practice of buying and selling indulgences in some parts of the Church. He translated the Bible from Latin into German to make it more accessible to ordinary people and challenged the authority of the Pope, believing instead that the Bible alone is the only source of divinely revealed authority. Luther also claimed that having a belief in God was enough to be saved from sin, whereas Catholics believe good deeds, celebrating the sacraments and living a faithful life are also essential for salvation. This marked a clear difference between the Catholic faith and Protestant beliefs. Luther gathered a strong following within Germany where he set up the Lutheran Church. The thinking of Luther and others, such as John Calvin, led to other new Protestant Churches and marked the beginning of a period of religious wars across the whole of Europe. It also led the reformers in some places to destroy the internal decorations of medieval Cathedrals, because they believed that having images in churches was against the teaching of the Bible.

▲ An eighteenth-century illustration of the Council of Trent; the council condemned Protestant teachings as heresy

The Catholic Church was very concerned about the Reformation and called the Council of Trent in 1543 as part of the Counter-Reformation. The Council condemned Protestant teachings as heresy, reinforcing Catholic teachings on the Bible, the sacraments, and salvation. It restated what the Church has always taught: that revelation came from scripture *and* tradition. Despite the efforts of the Church to resist the Reformation, it ultimately led to a schism in European Christianity that led to the existence of many different Churches, lots of which are still present in the world today.

From the very beginning of the Reformation there were further splits within the Protestant movement in Europe, leading to the emergence of many different Christian Churches. For example, while Calvin and Luther had many beliefs in common, their followers were in conflict with each other and wanted to remain separate, leading to Lutheranism and Calvinism. In England, Henry VIII's disagreement with the Pope led to the English Reformation and the establishment of the Church of England. Protestantism has led to the emergence of different ideas and beliefs and to the establishment of many different Christian Churches who disagree with each other, as well as with the Catholic Church.

> ### Link
>
> Read pages 52–55 to remind yourself why Catholics believe the Pope has such authority, and to understand the importance of the magisterium, scripture and tradition to Catholics.

Understand

1 a State one disagreement that took place within the Church.

   b What was the cause of the disagreement?

   c What happened due to this disagreement?

   d How has this led to different Christian groups forming?

Discern

2 'The Council of Trent was correct to reject Luther's idea that the Bible alone should be recognised as the source of Christian authority.' Do you agree? Explain your reasoning, and try to include a reference to a Bible teaching in your answer. You could reread pages 52–55 to help you answer this question.

3 'In matters of religious faith, it is impossible for everyone to agree – that is why we have so many Christian denominations.' How far do you agree with this statement? To support your answer, try explaining some of the differences between Protestant and Catholic beliefs.

Respond

4 Have you ever held an opinion that is different from how the majority of your friends think? Did it make you doubt yourself, or believe more strongly?

WHAT IS ECUMENISM?

OBJECTIVES

In this lesson you will explore **what is meant by ecumenism, its importance and the ways in which Christians work towards Christian unity.**

Today, there are many Christian denominations, who all hold different beliefs. However, each Christian group shares core beliefs which unite them as Christians: belief in one God, who is Father, Son and Holy Spirit; that Jesus died to bring about the salvation of the world; and the importance of the Bible. It can be easy to overlook these similarities and focus on the differences, yet Christians believe that **Christian unity** is essential.

What is ecumenism?

In Christianity, the term '**ecumenism**' has been used to describe the unity of all those who belong to the Christian faith across the world. Today, ecumenism is a movement to unite people from different Christian denominations so they can work together despite their differences. It is a form of reconciliation, meaning it tries to overcome differences, removing barriers to unity. In this way, ecumenism follows in the footsteps of Jesus, who Christians believe is the greatest reconciler. Through his sacrifice on the cross, Christians believe Jesus reconciled humanity with God.

'The restoration of unity among all Christians' was one of the key aims of the Second Vatican Council. The Catechism describes the importance of ecumenism:

> " 'the desire to recover the unity of all Christians is a gift of Christ and a call of the Holy Spirit'
>
> *Catechism of the Catholic Church 820*

This means that Jesus, through his actions, called for one united Church, but throughout the years this has not happened, therefore the Holy Spirit calls Christians to create Christian unity so Christianity can be as Jesus intended.

What do Christians need to do to bring about Christian unity?

At the centre of the ecumenical movement is Jesus and his call for unity. The Church teaches that:

> " '…in word and deed we must obey Christ, who expressly wills "that they may all be one" (Jn 17:21)'
>
> *Youth Catechism 131*

This means that to achieve ecumenism, Christians must agree to work together despite their differences and focus on what they have in common – a belief in, and worship of, the Trinitarian God. If all Christians did this, the possibility that the Church might be one again becomes a realistic hope. It also means that bringing about unity is the responsibility of all Christians because it is bringing about the Christianity that Jesus wanted.

Useful vocabulary

Christian unity: all Christians are united in common beliefs such as the importance of Jesus and his teachings

ecumenism: the aim of promoting unity among the Christian Churches of the world

Body of Christ: a name used by St Paul for the Church, the community of Christian believers who are spiritually connected and led by Jesus

common good: the idea that all people in society and the wider world should have everything that they need to thrive

Christians believe that they are all connected through the **Body of Christ**. They believe it is important to bring about unity as divisions within Christianity can hurt or damage the Body of Christ. There must be dialogue between Christian groups to help bring about understanding. Common prayer and worship are also seen as key because they remind people of the purpose of Christianity: to be a true disciple of Christ. Different Christian groups may share the same place of worship and take part in ecumenical services, where they worship together. The experience of praying together helps to remind Christians of all kinds about what they hold in common. These actions must be fully supported by leaders in the Church for the goal of Christian unity to succeed.

▲ *Different Christian groups can worship together at ecumenical services*

How do Christians work together to bring about the common good?

Christians believe they should work towards the **common good**, a world where everyone has what they need to thrive. This belief is central to Christianity because it is working to bring about the kingdom that Jesus proclaimed. There are many ways different Christian groups work towards the common good. The World Council of Churches is a community of Churches from around the world whose focus is to bring about ecumenism. They organise initiatives such as The Ecumenical Water Network. Many people in the world have limited access to water, so this initiative works to preserve water and make sure that it is fairly distributed. Another example is Food for Life, which works to ensure that people have food systems which are sustainable. Projects like these are an essential part of uniting Christianity as one faith, with Jesus' teachings at their core. They highlight the common beliefs of all Christians: human life is sacred; creation is a gift for all to share; and humans are made in the image of God and so should be treated with respect. Focusing on similarities rather than differences helps Christians to work together for the good of others.

Understand

1 What does ecumenism mean?
2 Describe two ways in which Christians can work towards ecumenism.
3 What does the term 'common good' mean for Christians?

Discern

4 Investigate ways in which different Christian groups work together for the common good in your local community. How does what they do bring about the common good? Do you have any ideas about what more could be done in your community to bring this about?

5 Consider the quote 'in word and deed we must obey Christ who expressly wills "that they may all be one"'. Choose one way in which Christians could respond to this teaching and work towards unity. Why you think this would be effective?

Respond

6 Do you have opportunities to speak with people in your community who have different religious beliefs to you? What does it mean to you to be able to do this? Is there anything that stops this from happening?

ASSESSMENT

Key vocabulary

Write a definition for these key terms.

ecumenical council   schism   dogma

reform   Christian unity   ecumenism

Knowledge check

1 Which of these phrases explains an ecumenical council?

  a A national meeting of Church leaders in a particular country

  b A worldwide meeting of the bishops of the Church at the invitation of the Pope

  c A local gathering of people to discuss issues in the local area

2 Copy out and complete the following sentence:

The Reformation in England led to the formation of the C.................. of E..................

3 What was the purpose of the First Council of Nicaea?

  a To state that Jesus was not divine

  b To clarify that Jesus was fully divine

  c To state that Jesus was created by God the Father

4 What is meant by the term 'gentile'?

5 The Catholic Church is often referred to as the 'universal Church'. What is meant by this?

6 Explain the purpose of the Council of Chalcedon.

7 Explain one reason why the Protestant Reformation took place.

8 What was the Council of Jerusalem and why was it important?

9 What is meant by the term 'ecumenism'? How does this connect all Christians?

10 Describe what Christians need to do to bring about ecumenism.

TIP

Think about the definition of ecumenism to help you get started. How can Christians work together to bring it about?

GLOSSARY

The words in **red** are Key Vocabulary terms from the Religious Education Directory.

A

Acts of the Apostles: a book in the New Testament which describes the beginning of the early Church, similar in style to a Gospel

Anglican: relating to the Church of England or the Anglican Communion – the worldwide group of Churches that follow Anglicanism and grew out of the Church of England. They are united under the guidance of the Archbishop of Canterbury

apostles: important early Christian teachers or missionaries, who Jesus sent to spread the Good News; the twelve chief disciples of Jesus

Aramaic: a language spoken by Jesus, and in the area where he grew up; some books of the Bible were written in Aramaic

Arianism: the belief put forward by Arius in the fourth century that Jesus was not divine

B

Bible: the Christian holy book

biblical idiom: a figurative phrase connected to a passage from the Bible which has a non-literal meaning

Big Bang theory: the scientific theory that the universe was formed through the expansion of a hot, dense point of energy

bishop: the head of a local area in the Catholic Church (called a diocese), who continues the work of the apostles

Blessed Sacrament: a term that refers to the body and blood of Jesus in the Eucharist

Body of Christ: one of the names of the Church, emphasising the community of all those who are members of Christ's body through Baptism, with Jesus as their head, working together like one body

C

canon (of scripture): the agreed list of books that make up the Catholic Bible

Catechism of the Catholic Church: a book summarising the official teachings of the Catholic Church

Catholic Social Teaching: the principles that Catholics should use to guide their behaviour, such as caring for the dignity of the human person or working for the common good

chaplain: a priest who is appointed to offer spiritual support to people in a particular organisation

Christ: a title for Jesus, which means he was chosen by God

Christian unity: all Christians are united in common beliefs such as the importance of Jesus and his teachings

Christmas: a Christian festival that celebrates the Incarnation in the birth of Jesus

common good: the idea that all people in society and the wider world should have everything that they need to thrive

Confirmation: the Sacrament of Initiation that completes Baptism and strengthens a person's faith by being sealed with the Holy Spirit as a mature member of the Church

congregation: the people who attend a service of worship

consecrated: blessed and made holy

consubstantiation: a Protestant belief that the bread and wine exist together with the body and blood of Christ in the consecrated Eucharist

Corpus Christi: the Latin phrase for 'body of Christ'; a feast that celebrates the Real Presence of Christ in the Blessed Sacrament

covenant: an agreement or promise between two or more people; God made covenants with humans such as Abraham and Moses

creatio ex nihilo: the Latin phrase for 'creation out of nothing'

creation: the act of bringing something into existence; or the universe and everything in it (which Catholics believe God created)

creationism: the belief that the Bible accounts of creation are literally true

D

Dei Verbum: the Latin phrase for 'Word of God'; also a document from the Second Vatican Council explaining how Jesus is the Word of God

denominations: branches of the Christian Church

deuterocanonical texts: a set of books in the Old Testament which are not part of the Jewish Tanakh or Protestant Old Testament

devotions: a religious practice which creates a feeling of love and commitment towards God

disciple: someone committed to following the teaching and example of Jesus

divine: of God

dogma: an essential belief which becomes a binding teaching in Catholicism

E

Eastern Orthodox: a branch of Christianity mainly, but not exclusively, found in Eastern Europe and the Middle East

ecumenical council: in Catholicism, a meeting of the bishops of the worldwide Church at the invitation of the Pope, to decide on matters of the Church.

ecumenism: the aim of promoting unity among the Christian Churches of the world

eschatology: the 'discussion of the last things', this includes death, Judgement, the soul and the end of time

eternal: exists beyond time and has no beginning or end

ethical: relating to moral principles or beliefs about what is right and wrong

Eucharist: the sacrament in which Catholics receive the body and blood of Christ; also called Holy Communion, the Lord's Supper, the Breaking of the Bread and Mass

evangelist: someone who spreads the Good News about Jesus; also the title used to refer to the four Gospel writers: Matthew, Mark, Luke and John

F

faith: personal commitment to God, which includes trusting and obeying God

friar: a religious brother who is a member of a mendicant order, for example the Franciscans, Dominicans, Augustinians or Carmelites

Fruit of the Mystery (of the Rosary): a virtue or behaviour that helps Catholics to grow in holiness

fruits of the Spirit: the behaviours and attitudes that are shown by a person who is filled with the Holy Spirit, such as love, joy and kindness

G

gifts of the Holy Spirit: seven spiritual gifts given by the Holy Spirit during the Sacrament of Confirmation: wisdom, understanding, counsel, might, knowledge, piety and fear of the Lord

God: the one supreme being, who creates and sustains everything

godparent: a practising Catholic, chosen to help nurture the faith of a person being baptised

Gospel: the term Gospel means 'Good News'; the Gospels are the books in the Bible that teach the Good News about Jesus

grace: a gift of love freely given by God to humankind

Great Commission: Jesus' instruction to the disciples to spread the Gospel to all nations of the world

Greek: a language spoken in Greece and throughout the Roman Empire; some books of the Bible were written in Greek

H

Hebrew: a language spoken by Jesus, and in the area where he grew up; some books of the Bible were written in Hebrew

heresy: an opinion or belief that goes against Church teaching, or the denial of a revealed truth

Holy Communion: another name for the Sacrament of Eucharist

Holy Spirit: the third person of the Trinity, true God, who Christians believe inspires people

host: the holy bread of the Eucharist

I

icon: a religious image, particularly popular in Orthodox Christianity, used for devotion or worship

imago Dei: a Latin phrase meaning 'in the image of God', the idea that humans reflect God's nature

immanent: operating in the universe; Catholics believe that God works within the universe to have a relationship with them and to sustain the universe

Incarnation: Christians believe that God became man in the person of Jesus, truly human and truly divine

indulgences: a way to reduce the amount of punishment given for sin

initiation: a ceremony to welcome or accept someone into an organisation

in persona Christi: Latin phrase for 'in the person of Christ'; the priest stands in the place of Jesus, who speaks through him during the Mass

inspired: 'God breathed'; the belief that the Holy Spirit guides a person to act or write what is good and true

Israelites: descendants of Jacob, later named Israel, whose life is described in the book of Genesis

J

Judaism: the religion of the Jewish people, who believe in one God, who revealed the Torah to Moses on Mount Sinai

L

Lamb of God: a title of Jesus linking his sacrifice on the cross to the sacrifice of the Passover lamb

Last Day of Judgement: the Jewish and Christian belief that there will be a day at the end of time when all people will be raised up and judged for their actions

lex orandi, lex credendi: Latin phrase meaning 'the law of prayer is the law of belief'

literary form: the style of writing used, for example a letter or a poem

literal sense: the meaning of the text as the author intended it to be; this is different to reading a passage literally which means accepting it as word-for-word truth

Liturgy of the Eucharist: the part of Mass where Catholics receive the body and blood of Christ

Liturgy of the Word: the part of Mass where the word of God is proclaimed (announced)

Lord: a person who has power and authority; a title for God in the Old Testament, also used for Jesus in the New Testament

Lord's Supper: another name for the Sacrament of Eucharist

M

magisterium: from the Latin term *magister*, meaning teacher or master; it is the authority of the Church to teach

martyr: someone who dies for their faith

Mass: the central act of worship for Catholics; one of the names for the Sacrament of the Eucharist

Messiah: a Hebrew term meaning 'anointed one'; many Jews interpret the 'Messiah' to be a future leader of the Jewish people who will rule with kindness and justice; for Christians the Messiah is Jesus; the word 'Christ' is the Greek form of the word Messiah

ministry: the work Jesus carried out to spread the word of God in the three years between his baptism and crucifixion

mission: a great task or purpose which, in Christianity, is given by God

monastery: a building or buildings where a community of religious brothers or sisters live

monotheistic: believing there is only one God

morals: standards of behaviour; knowing right from wrong

Mysteries of the Rosary: particular events in the life of Jesus or Mary, known as the Joyful, Sorrowful, Glorious and Luminous Mysteries

mystery: a truth, whose meaning will never be fully understood

N

New Testament: the books of the second half of the Bible, which tell the story of Jesus' life, ministry, death and resurrection, and the establishment of the early Church

O

OFM: Orders of Friars Minor, an abbreviation used after the name of certain Franciscan friars to show which order they are from

Old Testament: the books of the first half of the Bible showing the creation of the world and God's relationship with the Israelites

omnibenevolent: all loving

omnipotent: all powerful

P

Paschal Mystery: the belief that Jesus' death and resurrection brings salvation to every human being

Passover: a Jewish festival that celebrates God saving the Israelites from slavery in Egypt

Pentecost: a Christian festival celebrating the time when the Holy Spirit came down to the apostles; also a Jewish festival known as Shavuot, celebrating the harvest and the giving of the Torah at Mount Sinai

People of God: one of the names of the Church, emphasising the whole community of believers, united by their belief in God, the Father, Son and Holy Spirit

pilgrimage: a journey made for a spiritual purpose

Pope: the head of the Catholic Church, who continues as the successor of St Peter and is responsible for the emotional and spiritual needs of the Church

prayer: the way in which humans communicate with God

prophecies: God's messages for the world, warnings, encouragements or predictions

prophet: a person inspired by God through the Holy Spirit to share messages from God

Protestant: Christians who belong to any Church branch that protested against and separated from the Catholic Church following the Reformation in the sixteenth century

R

Real Presence: the belief that Jesus is really present in the celebration of the Eucharist, in which the bread and wine truly become his body and blood

reason: the ability to think in a clear and logical way

redemption: the belief that Jesus paid the 'ransom' to free humans from sin by dying on the cross

reform: to make changes to something

resurrection: the Christian belief that after his crucifixion and death, Jesus rose back to life

revelation: the way in which God is made known to humans, which Catholics believe is most perfectly done through Jesus

rite: a sacred act or ceremony

rosary beads: a string of beads used as an aid to prayer

ruah: a Hebrew word meaning wind or breath; God's Spirit that was breathed in Adam to bring him to full life

S

sacraments: visible signs of God's grace that make real what they symbolise; also the name given to the ceremonies that contain these signs

Sacrifice of the Mass: the belief that Jesus' sacrifice is really made present to Catholics during the Eucharist

saint: a person who is officially recognised by the Catholic Church as being very holy because of the way he or she lived, or died; also, anyone who is already in heaven, whether recognised or not

salvation: the process of being saved from sin and returning to God through his grace

sanctity: the state of being holy

schism: a split or division within a group

scientific theory: a commonly agreed idea, held by scientists and backed up by evidence

scientism: the belief that science can provide all of the answers in life

scripture: the holy book(s) of a religion; in Christianity it is the Bible

service: supporting the needs of others and putting them before your own; this might include physical and spiritual needs, for example

sin: to go against God's law

Son of God: a title of Jesus as the second person of the Trinity, reflecting his equal status to God the Father

Son of Man: a title for Jesus which suggests that he is both divine and human; it connects to the idea of him as a Messiah

sovereign: a ruler or leader of all

stewardship: the duty to care for something, in this case, the world and everything in it

sustainable: able to be kept going or maintained over time

sustainable development: carefully managing the use of the earth's resources so that they are not destroyed or used up as a result of human activities

T

Tanakh: the Jewish Bible

Temple of the Holy Spirit: one of the names of the Church, emphasising the community of all those who are led by God's spirit in their lives, given to them through the sacraments

theological: relating to the study of the nature of God and religious belief

theory of evolution: the scientific theory that every living thing changes, over a long period of time, to suit its environment

Torah: the first five books of the Jewish holy text, the Tanakh, which Jews believe were given to Moses by God

tradition: also known as Apostolic Tradition, these are actions and teachings of Jesus faithfully passed on through the sacraments and teachings of the Church

transcendent: existing outside of space and time

transubstantiation: the process by which the bread and wine actually become the body and blood of Jesus at the moment of consecration

Trinity: God as three in one – Father, Son and Holy Spirit

U

universal Church: the whole community of Catholics in the world

V

vows: solemn promises which cannot be broken

W

works of the flesh: human temptations or weaknesses such as jealousy, anger and envy

INDEX

ACKNOWLEDGEMENTS

The publisher and authors would like to thank the following for permission to use photographs and other copyright material:

Cover: Eleanor Grosch. **Photos: p10:** S-F / Shutterstock; **p13:** FatCamera / Getty Images; **p16:** Our Lady of Victories, Kensington; **p18:** Quality Stock Arts/Shutterstock; **p19:** Richard Lowthian / Shutterstock; **p21:** Granger Historical Picture Archive / Alamy Stock Photo; **p22:** Cosmin-Constantin Sava / 123RF; **p24(t):** St Vincent de Paul Society; **p24(b):** Chris Watt; **p25(t):** Thom Flint / CAFOD; **p25(b):** Pax Christi UK; **p26:** janrysavy / Getty Images; **p27:** AM113 / Shutterstock; **p28:** Art Directors & TRIP / Alamy Stock Photo; **p29:** Aubord Dulac / Shutterstock; **p31:** Amrit Rudro / CAFOD; **p32:** Creation, Donald Jackson with contributions from Chris Tomlin, © 2002 The Saint John's Bible, Saint John's University, Collegeville, Minnesota USA. Used by permission. All rights reserved; **p34:** Courtesy of the Sisters of Notre Dame de Namur; **p35:** worldclassphoto / Shutterstock; **p42:** motimeiri / iStock / Getty Images; **p44:** Godong / Universal Images Group / Getty Images; **p46:** jgroup / iStock/Getty Images; **p47:** 3bugsmom / iStock / Getty Images; **p48:** incamerastock / Alamy Stock Photo; **p51:** Tyler Olson / Shutterstock; **p52:** Renata Sedmakova / Shutterstock; **p55:** The History Collection / Alamy Stock Photo; **p56:** ColorBlind / Photodisc / Getty Images; **p57:** Pascal Deloche / Godong / Stone / Getty Images; **p60:** Ancient Art and Architecture / Alamy Stock Photo; **p63:** volkova natalia / Shutterstock; **p68:** meunierd / Shutterstock; **p70:** Keith McIntyre / Shutterstock; **p73:** imageBROKER / Alamy Stock Photo; **p75:** JESUS MAFA. Jesus heals a paralyzed man, from Art in the Christian Tradition, a project of the Vanderbilt Divinity Library, Nashville, TN.; **p77:** Radiant Light / Bridgeman Images; **p79:** Reed Kaestner / Getty Images; **p82:** robertharding / Alamy Stock Photo; **p85:** ABACA / Shutterstock; **p87:** Konstantin Zibert / Shutterstock; **p88:** PAINTING / Alamy Stock Photo; **p89:** Meg Wroe (www.megwroe.com); **p90:** ASP Religion / Alamy Stock Photo; **p91:** Jim Lord / Getty Images; **p96:** Romolo Tavani / Shutterstock; **p98:** Josh Applegate / Unsplash; **p99(t):** Sebastien Desarmaux / Getty Images; **p99(b):** Godong / Alamy Stock Photo; **p100:** WENN Rights Ltd / Alamy Stock Photo; **p102:** pmmart / Shutterstock; **p105:** Niday Picture Library / Alamy Stock Photo; **p106(l):** amer ghazzal / Alamy Stock Photo; **p106(r):** Miljan Zivkovic / Shutterstock; **p107(l):** Just dance / Shutterstock; **p107(r):** Godong / Universal Images Group via Getty Images; **p108:** Charles Walker Collection / Alamy Stock Photo; **p109:** Godong / Getty Images; **p110:** Mondadori Portfolio / Hulton Fine Art Collection / Getty Images; **p111:** jorisvo / Shutterstock; **p112:** Dan Kitwood / Getty Images; **p114:** MarioPonta / Alamy Stock Photo; **p115:** Marco Vacca / Getty Images; **p116:** Rungroj Yongrit / EPA / Shutterstock; **p117:** Coopération Internationale pour le Développement et la Solidarité; **p118:** JESUS MAFA. The Lord's Supper, from Art in the Christian Tradition, a project of the Vanderbilt Divinity Library, Nashville, TN.; **p119:** The Picture Art Collection / Alamy Stock Photo; **p120:** FooTToo / Shutterstock; **p121:** AGB Photo Library / Alamy Stock Photo; **p126:** jorisvo / Shutterstock; **p127:** duncan1890 / Getty Images; **p128(t):** Freepik Company; **p128(b):** marina_mikhaylova / Getty Images; **p129(a):** Trybex / Shutterstock; **p129(b):** StockFrame / Getty Images; **p129(c):** David Grossman / Alamy Stock Photo; **p129(d):** Prostock-studio / Shutterstock; **p129(e):** StockFrame / Getty Images; **p130:** jorisvo / Shutterstock; **p133:** Radiant Light / Bridgeman Images; **p135:** MissioUK; **p136:** Thoom / Shutterstock; **p139:** Mike Harrington / Getty Images; **p141:** John Leyba / The Denver Post via Getty Images; **p142:** Javier Cruz Acosta / Shutterstock; **p145:** Rawpixel.com / Shutterstock; **p146:** JESUS MAFA. Pentecost, from Art in the Christian Tradition, a project of the Vanderbilt Divinity Library, Nashville, TN.; **p148:** filmfoto / Getty Images; **p149:** Junita Bognanni; **p155:** Album / Alamy Stock Photo; **p157:** jozef sedmak / Alamy Stock Photo; **p159:** Heritage Image Partnership Ltd / Alamy Stock Photo; **p161:** Alessandra Benedetti – Corbis / Corbis via Getty Images.

Artwork by Eleanor Grosch, Dusan Lakicevic, Moreno Chiacchiera, and Kamae Design.

Every effort has been made to contact copyright holders of material reproduced in this book. Any omissions will be rectified in subsequent printings if notice is given to the publisher.

We are grateful to the authors and publishers for use of extracts from their titles and in particular the following:

Scripture quotations are from the ESV® Catholic Edition with Deuterocanonical Books (ESV-CE) copyright © 2017 by Crossway, a publishing ministry of Good News Publishers. Used by permission. All rights reserved. The ESV-CE text may not be quoted in any publication made available to the public by a Creative Commons license. The ESV-CE may not be translated in whole or in part into any other language. Users may not copy or download more than 500 verses of the ESV-CE Bible or more than one-half of any book of the ESV-CE Bible.

Extracts from **Catechism of the Catholic Church**, published by Vatican Publishing House. © Dicastero per la Comunicazione – Libreria Editrice Vaticana. Reproduced with permission by the Publisher.

Extracts from ***Dei Verbum***, published by Vatican Publishing House. © Dicastero per la Comunicazione – Libreria Editrice Vaticana. Reproduced with permission by the Publisher.

Extracts from ***Laudato si'***, published by Vatican Publishing House. © Dicastero per la Comunicazione – Libreria Editrice Vaticana. Reproduced with permission by the Publisher.

Extracts from **Youth Catechism of the Catholic Church**, published by Vatican Publishing House. © Dicastero per la Comunicazione – Libreria Editrice Vaticana. Reproduced with permission by the Publisher.

Extracts from ***Gaudium et Spes***, published by Vatican Publishing House. © Dicastero per la Comunicazione – Libreria Editrice Vaticana. Reproduced with permission by the Publisher.

CAFOD and Bangladesh Association for Sustainable Development (BASD) for information about southern Bangladesh eco-villages, 2022.

Excerpts from the English translation and chants of **The Roman Missal** © 2010, International Commission on English in the Liturgy Corporation. All rights reserved.

Thank you

This series is dedicated to Professor Anthony Towey – a friend
to all in RE. Your spirit, inspiration and legacy lives on in these
books.

Thank you to Mary Myatt who inspired us at the 2020 ATCRE
Conference to produce beautiful and ambitious books with
narrative at their heart.

Andy Lewis: To my Mum, Dad, Emily, Tommy and Joseph –
thank you for all your love, support and encouragement.

Rebecca Jinks: Thank you to my husband, Sean, and my sons
Isaac and Hugh who have been endlessly encouraging and
supportive of me, particularly in the writing of this book. To
them and my wider family, my colleagues at work and the team
at OUP, thank you for having faith in me.

Laura Howe: Thank you to my husband, Peter, for the
unwavering support he always gives. Thank you also to
my family for their love and encouragement. To my work
colleagues and the team at OUP, thank you for everything you
have done and continue to do.

Ann-Marie Bridle: Thank you to my husband Kevin for your
patience and support, and to my mum Philomena – between
them, they have helped me balance this project alongside
raising Liam and Lizzy. Liam and Lizzy, perhaps one day you will
read this resource for yourselves at school! Thank you to the
team at OUP for their kindness and proficiency throughout this
whole experience.

Mateusz Boniecki: Thank you to my wonderful wife, Olimpia,
without whose help my contribution would be impossible, and
to my son Octavian who, in his own unique way, encouraged
me in the writing. To my whole family, thank you for all your
kind words and love.

The publisher would like to thank the following people for their
contribution to the development of this book: Julia Naughton,
Harriet Power, Philip Robinson, Kathleen O'Brien and Susan
Kambalu at CAFOD, Julie Haigh, Rabbi Benjy Rickman, Revd Dr
Mark Griffiths, Fr Ian Graham. The publisher would also like to
thank James Helling for compiling the index for this book.